David Ross grew up in the eponymous county of Ross & Cromarty. He has written and edited many books on aspects of Scottish history and culture.

Scottish Quotations

Compiled and Edited by
David Ross

BIRLINN

This edition published in 2024 by
Birlinn Limited
West Newington House
10 Newington Road
Edinburgh
EH9 1QS

www.birlinn.co.uk

ISBN 978 1 78027 848 3

British Library Cataloguing-in-Publication Data
A catalogue record for this book is available
from the British Library.

Typeset by Mark Blackadder

Papers used by Birlinn Ltd are from well-managed
forests and other responsible sources

Printed and bound by Clays Ltd, Elcograf S.p.A.

Contents

Editor's Note   7

Advice, Aphorisms and Epithets   8
The Animal Kingdom   13
Art and Architecture   17
Boasts, Vaunts and Challenges   19
Robert Burns   21
Childhood   23
Commerce and Industry   25
Costume   27
Death   30
Education and Schools   34
Family and Social Life   36
Fantasy, Visions and Magic   38
Food and Drink   40
Human Nature   46
Lamentations   49
Landscape and Nature   53
The Law   56
Love   57
Men and Women   61
The Mind and Medicine   66
Mountains and Climbers   67
Music, Dance and Song   69
The People   71
Politics and Protest   74
Religion and Belief   78
Science and the Scientific Approach   87
The Sea and Seafaring   91
Seasons and Weather   93

Selves and Others   97
The Spirit of Scotland   107
Sports and Pastimes   113
Thoughts, Wishes and Reflections   118
Toasts and Greetings   124
Transport and Travel   126
War and Warriors   128
Words, Language and Speech   135
Work and Leisure   143
Writers and Readers   145
Youth and Age   154

Index of Persons Quoted   157

Editor's Note

The main purpose of this compilation is to provide a broad selection of interesting, entertaining, revealing and informative quotations from the writings and sayings of Scots through the centuries. Apart from any other uses, ranging as it does widely over topics and time, it also offers a way of exploring that many-faceted, multi-dimensional, semi-abstract organ, the Scottish mind – and of musing over how much, and how little, it has changed.

Advice, Aphorisms and Epithets

Don't quote your proverb until you bring your ship
into port.
Gaelic Proverb

Three things come without seeking – jealousy, terror and
love.
Traditional saying, from Gaelic

Ye'll be a man before your mither yet.
Anonymous, from Rob Roy MacGregor, *or* Auld Lang
Syne, *a musical show of 1819*

The wee man's gotten his parritch at last.
Anonymous, from Rob Roy MacGregor, *or* Auld Lang
Syne, *on the death of Rashleigh*

Gae seek your succour where ye paid blackmail.
Anonymous, Jamie Telfer in the Fair Dodhead

This Way is That Way. That Way is This Way.
Double signpost seen in a Scottish garden

a door never fully recovers from being opened with a boot.
Neal Ascherson (1932–), Stone Voices

You have been warned against letting the golden hours slip
by. Yes, but some of them are golden only because we let
them slip.
*Sir J.M. Barrie (1860–1937), Rectorial Address,
St Andrews University*

We can pay our debts to the past by putting the future in
debt to ourselves.
*John Buchan (1875–1940), Coronation address to the
people of Canada, 1937*

A fool and his money are soon parted.
Attributed to George Buchanan (c.1506–1582)

Nae man can tether time nor tide.
Robert Burns (1759–1796), Tam O'Shanter

For a' that, and a' that,
It's comin yet for a' that,
That Man to Man, the world o'er,
Shall brothers be, for a' that.
Robert Burns, A Man's a Man for a' That

Heaven can boil the pot
Tho' the Deil piss in the fire
Robert Burns, The Dean of Faculty

Facts are chiels that winna ding
And daurna be disputed
Robert Burns, A Dream

I dare not speak for mankind
I know so little of myself
John Burnside (1955–), Landscapes

Winning isn't everything. There should be no conceit in
victory and no despair in defeat.
Sir Matt Busby (1909–1994)

When one has been threatened with a great injustice, one
accepts a smaller as a favour.
Jane Welsh Carlyle (1801–1866), Diary, *November 1855*

He that has a secret should not only hide it, but hide that
he has something to hide.
Thomas Carlyle (1795–1881), The French Revolution

Happy the people whose annals are blank in history.
Thomas Carlyle, Frederick the Great

To a shower of gold, most things are penetrable.
Thomas Carlyle

Never trust a man who, left alone with a tea cosy in a
room, doesn't try it on.
  Sir Billy Connolly (1942–)

Timid souls are always in a hurry.
  John Davidson (1857–1909), Godfrida

Unless a man undertakes more than he can possibly do, he
will never do all he can do.
  Henry Drummond (1851–1897)

The man who is intent on making the most of his
opportunities is too busy to bother about luck.
  Bertie Charles Forbes (1890–1954), Forbes Epigrams

The Trick is to Keep Breathing
  Janice Galloway (1955–), book title

In Scotland, talking about yourself is considered the eighth
deadly sin.
  *Janice Galloway, at the Edinburgh International
  Book Festival, 2011*

It needs smeddum to be either right coarse or right kind.
  Lewis Grassic Gibbon (James Leslie Mitchell, 1901–1935),
  Smeddum

They loved this state; it kept them warm; it saved them
trouble; and they enshrined their tastes in their sayings –
'the mair dirt the less hurt', 'the clartier the cosier' …
Another saying was 'Muck makes luck'.
  H. Grey Graham, The Social Life of Scotland in the
  Eighteenth Century *(1899)*

Who has enough, of no more has he need.
Robert Henryson (c.1425–1500), The Town Mouse and the Country Mouse

That action is best, which procures the greatest happiness for the greatest numbers.
Francis Hutcheson (1694–1746), An Inquiry into the Original of Our Ideas of Beauty and Virtue

If folk think I'm mean, they'll no' expect too much.
Sir Harry Lauder (1870–1950), quoted in Albert Mackie, The Scotch Comedians

Men are immortal till their work is done.
David Livingstone (1813–1873), Letters

Experience teaches that it doesn't.
Norman MacCaig (1910–1996), Bruce and That Spider – the Truth

Beauty and sadness always go together.
George Macdonald (1852–1905), Within and Without

There is hope in honest error; none in icy perfection.
Charles Rennie Mackintosh (1868–1928)

Men are never so good or so bad as their opinions.
Sir James Mackintosh (1765–1832), Ethical Philosophy

It's a small world but I wouldn't want to have to paint it.
Chic Murray (1919–1985)

Truth will stand when a' thin's failin'
Lady Nairne (1766–1845), Caller Herrin'

Fate's book, but my italics.
Don Paterson (1963–)

We are all in the stars,
but some of us are
looking at the gutter.
Walter Perrie (1949–), Proverb

Sorrows remembered sweeten present joy.
Robert Pollok (1798–1827), The Course of Time

Behave yoursel' before folk;
What'er ye do, when out o' view,
Be cautious aye before folk.
Alexander Rodger (1784–1846),
Behave Yoursel' Before Folk

I always say appearance is only sin deep.
Saki (H.H. Munro, 1870–1916)

It's the early Christian that gets the fattest lion.
Saki, Reginald's Choir Treat

A little inaccuracy sometimes saves tons of explanation.
Saki, The Square Egg

Scandal is merely the compassionate allowance which the
gay make to the humdrum. Think how many blameless
lives are brightened by the indiscretions of other people.
Saki

A place for everything, and everything in its place.
Samuel Smiles (1812–1904), Thrift

Some folks are wise, and some are otherwise.
Tobias Smollett (1721–1771),
The Adventures of Roderick Random

'Dark glasses hide dark thoughts.' I said.
'Is that a saying?'
'Not that I've heard. But it is one now.'
Muriel Spark (1918–2006), The Dark Glasses

Whoever you pretend to be, you must face yourself eventually.
Al Stewart (1945–) Scottish-born US lyricist and musician

Better to love in the lowliest cot
Than pine in a palace alone.
George Whyte-Melville (1821–1878), Chastelar

The Animal Kingdom

A goloch is an awesome beast,
Souple an' scaly,
Wi' a horny heid an' a hantle o' feet,
An' a forky tailie.
Traditional

Said the whitrick to the stoat,
'I see ye've on your winter coat;
I dinna see the sense ava!
Ye're shairly no expectin' snaw?'
J.K. Annand (1908–1993), Fur Coats

She had the fiercie and the fleuk,
The wheezloch and the wanton yeuk;
On ilka knee she had a breuk –
What ail'd the beast to dee?
Patrick Birnie (fl. 1660s), The Auld Man's Mear's Dead

I turned a grey stone over: a hundred forky-tails seethed
from under it like thoughts out of an evil mind.
George Mackay Brown (1921–1996), Five Green Waves

Wee sleeket, cow'rin, tim'rous beastie,
O, what a panic's in thy breastie!
Thou needna start awa sae hasty
Wi' bickerin' brattle!
I wad be laith to rin and chase thee,
Wi' murderin' pattle!
Robert Burns (1759–1796), To a Mouse

He was a gash and faithfu' tyke
As ever lap a sheugh or dyke.
    Robert Burns, The Twa Dogs

puddocks is nae fat they eesed tae be.
    J.M. Caie (1878–1949), The Puddock

A cat is the ideal literary companion. A wife, I am sure,
cannot compare except to her disadvantage. A dog is out of
the question … Its function is that of a familiar. It is at once
decorative – contemplative – philosophical, and it begets in
me great calm and contentment.
    William Y. Darling (1885–1962), 'Memoirs of a Bankrupt
    Bookseller', quoted in Hamish Whyte, The Scottish Cat
    (1987)

A stag of warrant, a stag, a stag,
A runnable stag, a kingly crop,
Brow, bay and tray and three on top,
A stag, a runnable stag.
    John Davidson (1857–1909), A Runnable Stag

I have never yet met anyone who really believed in a
pterodactyl; but every honest person believes in dragons.
    Kenneth Grahame (1859–1932), Introduction to 100
    Fables of Aesop

I'm a cat, I'm a cat, I'm a Glesga cat and my name is Sam
the Skull, I've got claws in my paws like a crocodile's jaws
and a heid like a fermer's bull.
    Harry Hagan (1939–), Sam the Skull, *from Ewen*
    McVicar, gallusglasgowsongs website

When three hens go a-walking, they
Observe this order and array:
The first hen walks in front, and then
Behind her walks the second hen,
While, move they slow or move they fast,
You find the third hen walking last.
>   *Henry Johnstone (1844–1931)*, When Three Hens Go
>   Walking (*version of a French comptine*)

She flowed through fences like a piece of black wind
>   *Norman MacCaig (1910–1996)*, Praise of a Collie

The collie underneath the table
Slumps with a world-rejecting sigh.
>   *Norman MacCaig*, Crofter's Kitchen, Evening

Above all, I love them because,
Pursued in water, they never
panic so much that they fail
to make stylish triangles
with their ballet dancer's
legs.
>   *Norman MacCaig*, Frogs

And shambles-ward nae cattle-beast e'er passes
But I mind hoo the saft e'en o' the kine
Lichted Christ's cradle wi' their canny shine.
>   *Hugh MacDiarmid (C.M. Grieve, 1892–1978)*,
>   Gairmscoile

A bird knows nothing of gladness,
Is only a song-machine.
>   *George Macdonald (1824–1905)*, A Book of Dreams

And houseless slugs, white, black and red –
Snails too lazy to build a shed.
>   *George Macdonald*, Little Boy Blue

The four-legged brain of a walk-ecstatic dog
    Harold Monro (1879–1932), Dog

… the cat is grown small and thin with desire,
Transformed to a creeping lust for milk.
    Harold Monro, Milk for the Cat

Though frail as dust it meet thine eye,
He form'd this gnat who built the sky.
    James Montgomery (1771–1854), The Gnat

'The Congo's no' to be compared wi' the West o' Scotland
when ye come to insects,' said Para Handy. 'There's places
here that's chust deplorable whenever the weather's the
least bit warm. Look at Tighnabruaich! – they're that bad
there, they'll bite their way through corrugated iron roofs to
get at ye!'
    Neil Munro (1864–1930), The Vital Spark

Up frae the rashes, heich abune the trees,
Intil the lift wi eldrich skraich an cletter,
In thair ticht squadrons tovin,
the wild geese I watch in joy
wing frae the braid lown watter.
    William Neill (1922–2010), On Loch Ken Side

… those poor souls who claim
to own a cat, who long to recognise
in bland and narrowing eyes a look like love,
are bound to suffer.
    Alastair Reid (1926–2014), Propinquity

My ewie wi' the crookit horn!
A' that kend her would hae sworn
Sic a ewie ne'er was born
Hereabouts nor far awa'.
    John Skinner (1721–1807),
    The Ewie wi' the Crookit Horn

The friendly cow, all red and white,
I love with all my heart;
She gives me cream with all her might,
To eat with apple-tart.
  Robert Louis Stevenson (1850–1894), The Cow

... a diminutive she-ass, not much bigger than a dog, the
colour of a mouse, with a kindly eye and determined
under-jaw. There was something neat and high-bred, a
quakerish elegance, about the rogue that hit my fancy on
the spot.
  Robert Louis Stevenson, Travels with a Donkey

Who's that ringing at our door-bell?
'I'm a little black cat and I'm not very well.'
Then rub your little nose with a little mutton fat,
And that's the best cure for a little black cat.
  Sir D'Arcy Wentworth Thompson (1860–1948),
  The Little Black Cat

... does it make for death to be
Oneself a living armoury?
  Andrew Young (1885–1971), The Dead Crab

There are all sorts of cute puppy dogs, but it doesn't stop
people from going out and buying Dobermans.
  Angus Young (1959–)

Art and Architecture

It's grand, and you cannot expect to be baith grand and
comfortable.
  Sir J.M. Barrie (1860–1937), The Little Minister

... a jewel of great price: St Magnus Cathedral ...
Unmoving, still it voyages on, the great ark of the people of
Orkney, into unknown centuries.
  George Mackay Brown (1921–1996), An Orkney Tapestry

This mony a year I've stood the flood an' tide:
And tho' wi' crazy eild I'm sair forfairn,
I'll be a brig when ye're a shapeless cairn.
Robert Burns (1759–1796), The Brigs of Ayr

They gazed with blanched faces at the House with the
Green Shutters, sitting there dark and terrible, beneath the
radiant arch of dawn.
George Douglas (George Douglas Brown, 1869–1902),
The House with the Green Shutters

I might not know what art is but I'll milk it for all it's
worth.
*Glasgow civic leader, paraphrased by James Kelman in a
lecture at Glasgow School of Art, 1996*

Bungalows ... the ceilings are so low, all you can have for
tea is kippers.
Anonymous, quoted in Charles McKean, Thirties Scotland

All great and living architecture has been the direct
expression of the needs and beliefs of man at the time of its
creation, and now, if we would have good architecture
created, this should still be so.
Charles Rennie Mackintosh (1868–1928), Lectures and
Notes

There are many decorative features in Scottish architecture
which might well be replaced by others of antiquity, but
because we are Scottish and not Greek or Roman, we reject
... I think we should be a little less cosmopolitan and rather
more national in our architecture.
Charles Rennie Mackintosh, Lectures and Notes

Abbotsford is a very strange house ... that it should ever
have been lived in is the most astonishing, staggering,
saddening thing of all. It is surely the strangest and saddest
monument that Scott's genius created.
Edwin Muir (1887–1959), Scottish Journey

A Celtic-Catalan cocktail to blow both minds and budgets.
Catherine Slessor, Architectural Review, *on the Holyrood Parliament building, 2004*

A hoose is but a puppet-box
To keep life's images frae knocks,
But mannikins scrieve oot their sauls
Upon its craw-steps and its walls:
Whaur hae they writ them mair sublime
Than on yon gable-ends o' time?
Lewis Spence (1874–1955), The Prows o' Reekie

Day by day, one new villa, one new object of offence, is added to another; all around Newington and Morningside, the dismalest structures keep springing up like mushrooms; the pleasant hills are loaded with them, each impudently squatted in its garden ... They belong to no style of art, only to a form of business.
Robert Louis Stevenson (1850–1894), Picturesque Notes on Edinburgh

A statement of sparkling excellence
Judges of the Stirling Prize, on the Holyrood Parliament building, 2004

No art that is not intellectual can be worthy of Scotland. Bleak as are her mountains, and homely as are her people, they have yet in their habits and occupations a characteristic acuteness and feeling.
Sir David Wilkie (1785–1841), from a speech made in Rome, 1827

Boasts, Vaunts and Challenges

I never will turn: do you think I will fly?
But here will I ficht, and here I will die.
Anonymous, The Baron of Brackley

My hands are tied, but my tongue is free
Anonymous, Kinmont Willie

I can drink and nae be drunk,
I can fecht and nae be slain;
I can lie wi another man's lass
And aye be welcome tae my ain.
Traditional, The Barnyards o' Delgaty

Whaur's yer Wullie Shakespeare noo?
Over-excited theatre-goer at the first night of John Home's play Douglas, *December 1756*

Here's tae us – Wha's like us?
Damn few – and they're a' deid.
Traditional

The Scottish Parliament adjourned on the 25th day of March 1707 is hereby reconvened.
Winnie Ewing (1929–2023), Acting President of the Scottish Parliament, 1 July 1999

I on the other hand would sacrifice a million people any day for one immortal lyric. I am a scientific socialist.
Hugh MacDiarmid (C.M. Grieve, 1892–1978), Scottish Scene

Och hey! for the splendour of tartans!
And hey for the dirk and the targe!
The race that was hard as the Spartans
Shall return again to the charge.
Pittendrigh MacGillivray (1856–1930), The Return

He either fears his fate too much,
Or his deserts are small,
That puts it not unto the touch,
To win, or lose, it all.
Marquis of Montrose (1612–1650), To His Mistress

'Behold the Tiber!' the vain Roman cried,
Viewing the ample Tay from Baiglie's side;
But where's the Scot that would the vaunt repay,
And hail the puny Tiber for the Tay?
　　Sir Walter Scott (1771–1832), The Fair Maid of Perth

Sound, sound the trumpet, sound the fife,
Loud the glorious truth proclaim:
One crowded hour of glorious life
Is worth an age without a name
　　Sir Walter Scott

'And oh, man,' he cried in a kind of ecstasy, 'am I no a
bonny fighter?'
　　Robert Louis Stevenson (1850–1894), Kidnapped

I have taken a firm resolution to conquer or to die and stand
my ground as long as I have a man remaining with me.
　　Prince Charles Edward Stuart (1720–1788), letter to his
　　father, 1745

The Minister said it wald dee,
the cypress buss I plantit.
But the buss grew til a tree,
naething dauntit.
It's growan, stark and heich,
derk and straucht and sinister,
kirkyairdie-like and dreich.
But whaur's the Minister?
　　Douglas Young (1913–1973), Last Lauch

Robert Burns

What an antithetical mind! – tenderness, roughness –
delicacy, coarseness, – sentiment, sensuality – soaring and
grovelling, dirt and deity – all mixed up in that one
compound of inspired clay.
　　Lord Byron (1788–1824), Journal, *1813*

A Burns is infinitely better educated than a Byron.
Thomas Carlyle (1795–1881), Note Book

In a life-long crucifixion Burns summed up what the common poor man feels in widely-severed moments of exaltation, insight and desperation.
Catherine Carswell (1879–1946), The Life of Robert Burns

No' wan in fifty kens a wurd Burns wrote,
But misapplied is a'body's property ...
Hugh MacDiarmid (C.M. Grieve 1892–1978),
A Drunk Man Looks at the Thistle

... the greatest peasant – next perhaps to King David of the Jews, a peasant, a poet, a patriot and a king – whom any age had produced.
Charles Mackay (1814–1889), Forty Years' Recollections of Life, Literature, and Public Affairs

He has the power of making any Scotsman, whether generous or canny, sentimental or prosaic, religious or profane, more wholeheartedly himself than he could have been without assistance; and in that way perhaps more human.
Edwin Muir (1887–1959), Essays on Literature and Society

... he was always with me, for I had him by heart ...
Wherever a Scotsman goes, there goes Burns. His grand, whole, catholic soul squares with the good of all; therefore we find him in everything everywhere.
John Muir (1838–1914), *'Thoughts on the Birthday of Robert Burns', from L.M. Wolfe*, John of the Mountains: The Unpublished Journals of John Muir

Childhood

Oh, will ye never learn?
Ne'er, ne'er was sic a bairn.
Breakin' my heart, ye fidgety, fidgety,
Breakin' my heart, ye fidgety bairn.
    Anonymous, Ye Fidgety Bairn

They never heed a word I speak;
I try to gie a froon,
But aye I hap them up an' cry,
'O, bairnies, cuddle doon.'
    Alexander Anderson ('Surfaceman', 1845–1900),
    Cuddle Doon

Stir the fire till it lowes, let the bairnie sit,
Auld Daddy Darkness is no wantit yet.
    James Ferguson (fl. 19th century), Auld Daddy Darkness

You only need to spend an afternoon with a child to realise
that most of them, without even trying, are poets.
    Janice Galloway (1955–), interview with Kirstin Innes,
    The List, *4 September 2008*

These children are happy.
It is easier for them.
They are English.
    Alasdair Gray (1934–2019), The Fall of Kelvin Walker

Where the pools are bright and deep,
Where the grey trout lies asleep,
Up the river and over the lea,
That's the way for Billy and me.
    James Hogg (1770–1835), A Boy's Song

Because if it ever came to the choice between living and dying then christ almighty he would lay down his life and glad to do it. They were great wee weans. Great wee weans. Even if they were horrible wee weans and selfish and spoilt brats he would still have done it.
James Kelman (1946–), A Disaffection

From the moment of birth, when the Stone Age baby confronts the twentieth-century mother, the baby is subjected to these forces of violence, called love, as its father and mother and their parents and their parents before them, have been.
R.D. Laing (1927–1989), The Politics of Experience

We are children, but some day
We'll be big, and strong, and say
None shall slave and none shall slay –
Comrades all together.
Socialist Sunday School hymn, from Jennie Lee (1904–1988), Tomorrow is a New Day

Gin they wad leave me alane!
Alastair Mackie (1925–1995), Adolescence

Wee Willie Winkie rins through the toun,
Upstairs and doun stairs in his nicht-gown,
Tirling at the window, crying at the lock:
Are a' the bairnies in their bed, it's past ten o'clock?
William Miller (1810–1872), Wee Willie Winkie

We tell our children they're trapped like rats on a doomed, bankrupt, gangster-haunted planet with dwindling resources, with nothing to look forward to but rising sea levels and imminent mass extinctions, then raise a disapproving eyebrow when, in response, they dress in black, cut themselves with razors, starve themselves, gorge themselves, or kill one another.
Grant Morrison (1960–)

Just at the age 'twixt boy and youth,
When thought is speech, and speech is truth.
  Sir Walter Scott (1771–1832), Marmion

Aince upon a day my mither said to me:
Dinna cleip and dinna rype
And dinna tell a lee.
  William Soutar (1898–1943), Aince Upon a Day

One's prime is elusive. You little girls, when you grow up,
must be on the alert to recognise your prime, at whatever
time of life it may occur.
  Muriel Spark (1918–2006),
  The Prime of Miss Jean Brodie

… all my pupils are the crème de la crème.
  Muriel Spark, The Prime of Miss Jean Brodie

A child should always say what's true,
And speak when he is spoken to,
And behave mannerly at table;
At least as far as he is able.
  Robert Louis Stevenson (1850–1894), The Whole Duty of
  Children

as a child, I won prizes at school and my mother's reaction
was invariably: 'Very good, but don't tell folk – they'll think
you're boasting.'
  Alex Wood, headteacher, in Times Educational
  Supplement (Scotland), *1 December 2006*

Commerce and Industry

You are being paid as if you are superhuman, but you are
not.
  *Shareholder to Royal Bank of Scotland directors at its
  annual meeting, quoted in* The Guardian, *24 April 2008*

We will never return to the old boom and bust.
Gordon Brown (1951–), Budget speech, March 2007

We cam na here to view your warks,
In hopes to be mair wise,
But only, lest we gang to hell,
It may be no surprise.
Robert Burns (1759–1796), Impromptu on Carron Ironworks

Pioneering does not pay.
Andrew Carnegie, (1835–1918), quoted in Hendrick's
Life of Carnegie.

Put all your eggs in one basket, and then watch the basket.
Andrew Carnegie, quoted in Hendrick's Life of Carnegie

In every commercial state, notwithstanding any pretension
to equal rights, the exaltation of a few must depress the
many.
Adam Ferguson (1723–1816), Essay on the History of
Civil Society

When the historian knew of happenings calculated to cast
odium on our landed gentry, he carefully excised the
records, and where he did not know, he was careful to
assume, and lead others to assume, that the period of
which he was ignorant were periods of intense social
happiness, wherein a glad and thankful populace spent
their days and their nights in devising Hallelujahs in
honour of the neighbouring nobleman. And that is why the
history of Scots mining is wrapped in darkness.
Tom Johnston (1881–1965), Our Scots Noble Families

All you folks are off your head
I'm getting rich from your sea bed
I'll go home when I see fit
All I'll leave is a heap of shit
John McGrath (1935–2002), The Cheviot, the Stag and
the Black, Black Oil

I cannot sit still, James, and hear you abuse the shopocracy.
  Christopher North (John Wilson, 1785–1854), Noctes
  Ambrosianae

Historians will be puzzled by the Oil Phenomenon: how an
intelligent, well-educated nation in a developed country
became the only people ever to discover oil and become
poorer.
  Jim Sillars (1937–), Nationalist politician

It is not by augmenting the capital of the country, but by
rendering a greater part of that capital active and
productive than would otherwise be so, that the most
judicious operations of banking can increase the industry of
the country.
  Adam Smith (1723–1790), The Wealth Of Nations

To found a great empire for the sole purpose of raising up a
people of customers, may at first sight appear a project fit
only for a nation of shopkeepers
  Adam Smith, The Wealth Of Nations

All money is a matter of belief.
  Adam Smith

Everyone lives by selling something.
  Robert Louis Stevenson (1850–1894), Beggars

Costume

O laith, laith were our gude Scots lords
To wat their cork-heeled shoon,
But lang ere a' the play was play'd
They wat their hats aboon.
  Anonymous, Sir Patrick Spens

The kilt, being a practical outdoor garment, failed him only once, and that occurred during a short-lived interest in bee-keeping.

J.M. Bannerman (1901–1969), Bannerman: The Memoirs of Lord Bannerman of Kildonan

When I looked at myself in the glass last night in my Corsican dress, I could not help thinking your opinion of yourself might be yet more upraised: 'She has secured the constant affection and admiration of so fine a fellow.'

James Boswell (1740–1795), *letter to Margaret Montgomerie*

Her cutty sark, o' Paisley harn,
That while a lassie she had worn,
In longitude tho' sorely scanty,
It was her best, and she was vauntie.

Robert Burns (1759–1796), Tam O' Shanter

Friends! Trust not the heart of that man for whom Old Clothes are not venerable.

Thomas Carlyle (1795–1881), Sartor Resartus

Braid claith lends fowk an unco heese,
Makes many kail-worms butter-flees

Robert Fergusson (1750–1774), Braid Claith

… getting down on the floors to scrub would be an ill-like ploy, she would warrant, for the brave silk knickers that Mrs Colquhoun wore. For the Sourock's wife had never forgiven the minister's wife her bit under-things, and the way she voted at the General Election.

Lewis Grassic Gibbon (James Leslie Mitchell, 1901–1935), Cloud Howe

Do I like women's clothes more than their bodies? Oh, no, but I prefer their clothes to their minds. Their minds keep telling me, no thank you, don't touch, go away. Their clothes say, look at me, want me, I am exciting.

Alasdair Gray (1934–2019), 1982 Janine

'Whit will I wear under it?' I asked. Few of us in Lomond Street wore underpants. 'Soldiers don't wear anything under their kilts.' I wondered how she knew. But even if it was true, soldiers just had Boers shooting at them, they didn't have Jock Dempster or Rab McIntyre come whooping out of a close to snatch up their kilts and show their bums to lassies.

Robin Jenkins (1912–1992), Fergus Lamont

Sick and sore I am, worn and weary,
walking no more since my limbs are confined.
Cursed be the king who stretched our stockings,
down in the dust may his face be found.

*John MacCodrum (c.1693–1779), 'Oran Mu'n Eideadh
Ghaidhealach'* (Song to the Highland Dress)

My kilt and tartan stockings I was wearing,
My claymore and my dirk and skian-dhu,
And when I sallied forth with manly bearing
I heard admiring whispers not a few –
'He's the best-dressed Highlander,
The best-dressed Highlander,
The best-dressed Highlander at his own expense.'

D.M. McKay, The Best-Dressed Highlander, *c.1889*

Wi' shanks like that ye'd better hae stuck to breeks.
Charles Murray (1864–1941), Ay, Fegs

Her coats were kiltit, and did sweetly shaw
Her straight bare legs that whiter were than snaw;
Her cockernony snooded up fou' sleek,
Her haffet-locks hung waving on her cheek

Allan Ramsay (1686–1758), The Gentle Shepherd

His socks compelled one's attention without losing one's respect.
Saki (H.H. Munro, 1870–1916),
The Chronicles of Clovis

Two long and bony arms were terminated at the elbow by triple blond ruffles, and being folded saltire-ways in front of her person, and decorated with long gloves a bright vermillion colour, presented no bad resemblance to a pair of gigantic lobsters.

Sir Walter Scott (1771–1832), The Antiquary

Let others boast of philibeg,
Of kilt and tartan plaid,
Whilst we the ancient trews will wear,
In which our fathers bled.

Sir John Sinclair (1754–1835), March for the Rothesay
and Caithness Fencibles

The kilt is … I don't know how to put this … it's an aphrodisiac. I can't tell you why, but it works … hap your hurdies with the passion pleats and it doesn't seem to matter what kind of women they are – rich, poor, old, young, black, white and yellow – they just melt, go shoogly in the legs, and, well, submit … Unconditional surrender.

W. Gordon Smith (1928–1996), Mr Jock (1987)

Death

Remember man, as thou goes by,
As thou art now, so once was I;
As I am now so thou shalt be,
Remember man that thou must die.

*Inscription once mounted at the entrance to Greyfriars
Churchyard, Edinburgh*

I am washing the shrouds of the fair men
Who are going out but shall never come in;
The death-dirge of the ready-handed men
Who shall go out, seek peril, and fall.

Song of the River Sprite Nigheag, from Gaelic

Mony an ane for him maks mane
But nane sall ken where he is gane;
Ower his white banes when they are bare,
The wind sall blaw for evermair.
  Anonymous, The Twa Corbies

Death is the port where all may refuge find,
The end of labour, entry into rest.
  Sir William Alexander (c.1567–1640),
  The Tragedy of Darius

Beyond the ever and the never,
I shall be soon.
  Horatius Bonar (1808–1889),
  Beyond the Smiling and the Weeping

Now, God be with you, my children: I have breakfasted
with you and shall sup with my Lord Jesus Christ this
night.
  Robert Bruce of Kinnaird (1554–1631), on his death-bed

O Death! the poor man's dearest friend –
  Robert Burns (1759–1796), Man Was made to Mourn

Don't let the awkward squad fire over my grave.
  Robert Burns, quoted on his deathbed

To live in hearts we leave behind
Is not to die.
  Thomas Campbell (1777–1844), Hallowed Ground

He died, seated, with a bowl of milk on his knee, of which
his ceasing to live did not spill a drop, a departure which it
seemed, after the event happened, might have been
foretold of this attenuated philosophical gentleman.
  Henry Thomas Cockburn (1779–1854), Memorials, *on the
  death of Joseph Black*

Sen for the deid remeid is none,
Best is that we for deth dispone,
Eftir our deth that leif may we:
Timor mortis conturbat me.
William Dunbar (c.1460–c.1520),
Lament for the Deth of the Makkaris

Death is a grim creditor, and a doctor but brittle bail when
the hour o'reckoning's at han'!
John Galt (1779–1839), Annals of the Parish

What a pity it is, mother, that you're now dead, for here's
the minister come to see you.
John Galt, Annals of the Parish

God forbid that I should go to any heaven where there are
no horses.
*R.B. Cunninghame Graham (1852–1936), letter to
President Theodore Roosevelt*

Of kindelie death nane suld affraied be
But sich as hope for na felicitie.
Alexander Hume (c.1560–1609), To His Sorrofull Saull,
Consolatioun

I am dying as fast as my enemies, if I have any, could wish,
and as easily and cheerfully as my best friends could desire.
David Hume (1711–1776), recorded in William Smellie,
Literary and Characteristical Lives *(1800)*

If suicide be supposed a crime, it is only cowardice can
impel us to it. If it be no crime, both prudence and courage
should engage us to rid ourselves at once of existence when
it becomes a burden. It is the only way we can then be
useful to society
David Hume, Essays

Vain are all things when death comes to your door.
  Murdo Mackenzie (fl. 1650s), Diomhanas nan
  Diomhanas (*Vanity of Vanities*), *translated by William
  Neill*

Let children walk with nature, let them see the beautiful
blending and communion of death and life, their joyous
inseparable unity, as taught in woods and meadows, plains
and mountains and streams of our blessed star, and they
will learn that death is stingless indeed, and as beautiful as
life, and that the grave has no victory, for it never fights. All
is divine harmony.
  John Muir (1838–1914)

There's nae sorrow, there John,
There's neither cauld nor care, John,
The day is aye fair,
In the land o' the leal.
  Lady Nairne (1766–1845), The Land o' the Leal

Nae stroke o' fortune cloured wi' bloody claa,
Nor glow'ring daith wi' sudden tempest mocked,
But in his wee thatched croft he wore awa'
E'en as a cruisie flickers oot unslockt.
  Robert Rendall (1898–1967), The Fisherman

Under the wide and starry sky
Dig the grave, and let me lie.
Glad did I live and gladly die,
And I laid me down with a will.
  Robert Louis Stevenson (1850–1894), Requiem

Cruel as death, and hungry as the grave
  James Thomson (1700–1748), Winter

This little life is all we must endure,
The grave's most holy peace is ever sure,
We fall asleep and never wake again.
  James Thomson (1834–1882), The City of Dreadful Night

The restful rapture of the inviolate grave.
   James Thomson, To Our Ladies of Death

Education and Schools

Mr Rhind is very kind,
He goes to kirk on Sunday.
He prays to God to give him strength
To skelp the bairns on Monday.
   Old Children's Rhyme

The schoolmaster is abroad, and I trust to him, armed with
his primer, more than I do the soldier in full military array,
for upholding and extending the liberties of the country ...
Education makes a people easy to lead, but difficult to
drive; easy to govern but impossible to enslave.
   *Lord Brougham (1778–1868) speech to the House of
   Commons, 1828*

Experience is the best of schoolmasters, only the school-
fees are heavy.
   Thomas Carlyle (1795–1881), Miscellaneous Essays

There's nothing quite like a Scotch education. It leaves an
irrepayable debt. My head is still full of irregular verbs.
   Ivor Cutler (1923–2006)

When we make laws which compel our children to go to
school we assume collectively an awesome responsibility.
For a period of ten years ... our children are conscripts; and
their youth does nothing to alter the seriousness of this fact.
   Margaret C. Donaldson (1926–2020), Children's Minds

One of my greatest hopes from a Scottish parliament is the
advancement of education to the point at which my
Scottish students would speak to me.
   Douglas Dunn (1942–), quoted in Neal Ascherson,
   Stone Voices

A single excursion under sympathetic and intelligent guidance to an instructive quarry, river-ravine, or sea-shore, is worth many books and a long course of systematic lectures.
Sir Archibald Geikie (1835–1924),
My First Geological Excursion

Perhaps all teachers should pour fine stuff into children's ears and leave their memories to resurrect it when they find their own thoughts inadequate.
Alasdair Gray (1934–2019), 1982 Janine

The dawn of legibility in his handwriting has revealed his utter inability to spell.
Attributed to Ian Hay (John Hay Beith, 1876–1952)

... the schools are not on our side. They are the agencies of the rulers. They bring us up to do what we are told, and not to speak back, to learn our lessons and pass the examinations. Above all, not to ask questions.
R.F. Mackenzie (1910–1987), A Search for Scotland

There is never a problem child; there is only a problem parent.
A.S. Neill (1883–1973), The Problem Parent

A good teacher does not draw out: he gives out, and what he gives out is love.
A.S. Neill, The Problem Teacher

Good gracious, you've got to educate him first. You can't expect a boy to be vicious until he's been to a really good school.
Saki (H.H. Munro, 1870–1916)

Give me a girl at an impressionable age, and she is mine for life.
Muriel Spark (1918–2006),
The Prime of Miss Jean Brodie

Delightful task! To rear the tender thought,
To teach the young idea how to shoot.
  James Thomson (1700–1748), The Seasons

Family and Social Life

Ye daurna swear aboot the toon,
It is against the law,
An' if ye use profanities,
Then ye'll be putten awa'.
  Traditional, Drumdelgie

Fame is rot: daughters are the thing.
  Sir J.M. Barrie (1860–1937), Dear Brutus

'I' my grandfather's time, as I have heard him tell, ilka
maister o' a faamily had his ain sate in his ain hoose; aye,
an' sat wi' his hat on his heed afore the best in the land; an'
had his ain dish, an' wus aye helpit first, an' keepit up his
authority as a man should do. Paurents were paurents then
– bairns daurdna set upo' their gabs afore them as they dae
noo.'
  Susan Ferrier (1782–1854), Marriage

The awe and dread with which the untutored savage
contemplates his mother-in-law are amongst the most
familiar facts of anthropology.
  Sir James G. Frazer (1854–1941), The Golden Bough

I can make a lord, but only God Almighty can make a
gentleman.
  King James VI (1566–1625)

In circumstances roughly similar to this one, in certain
tribes of chimpanzees, individuals bare their arses to each
other, a method of pacifying the aggressor. But this wasnt
the place to display arses. This was family.
  James Kelman (1946–), A Disaffection

Poor mother, she thought, she's had five children and she's as barren as Rannoch Moor, What did she know of life with her church committees and her Madeira cakes and her husband who was more Calvinistic than Calvin himself?
Joan Lingard (1932–2022), The Prevailing Wind

And the atmosphere warm with that lovely heat,
The warmth of tenderness and loving souls, the smiling anxiety,
That rules a house where a child is about to be born.
Hugh MacDiarmid (C.M. Grieve, 1892–1978),
Lo! A Child is Born

Women do not find it difficult nowadays to behave like men, but they often find it extremely difficult to behave like gentlemen.
Compton Mackenzie (1883–1972), Literature in My Time

You waitit for me to be born
I wait for you to dee.
Alastair Mackie (1925–1995), For My Father

Marriage is one long conversation, chequered by disputes.
Robert Louis Stevenson (1850–1894)

Matrimony … no more than a sort of friendship recognised by the police.
Robert Louis Stevenson

My children from the youngest to the eldest loves me and fears me as sinners dread death. My look is law.
Lady Strange, quoted in H.G. Graham, The Social Life of Scotland in the Eighteenth Century *(1899)*

She thought that her relatives were so boring. They hung onto the mundane for grim life; it was a glum adhesive binding them together.
Irvine Welsh (1957–), Trainspotting

Fantasy, Vision and Magic

The cock doth craw, the day doth daw,
The channerin' worm doth chide
    Anonymous, The Wife of Usher's Well

Then up and crew the milk white cock,
And up and crew the grey,
Her lover vanished in the air,
And she gaed weeping away.
    Anonymous, Clerk Saunders

'And see ye not that bonnie road
That winds about the ferny brae?
That is the road to fair Elfland,
Where thou and I this night maun gae.'
    Anonymous, Thomas the Rhymer

She cam' tripping adown the stair,
And a' her maids before her;
As soon as they saw her weel-faur'd face,
They cast the glamourie owre her.
    Anonymous, Johnnie Faa

'I saw the new moon late yestreen,
Wi' the auld moon in her arm;
And if we gang to sea, master,
I fear we'll come to harm.'
    Anonymous, Sir Patrick Spens

Yit scho wanderit and yeid by to ane elriche well,
Scho met thar, as I wene,
Ane ask rydand on a snaill,
And cryit, 'Ourtane fallow, haill!'
And raid ane inch behind the taill,
Till it wes neir evin.
    William Dunbar (c.1459–c.1530), Kynd Kittok

The shore was cold with mermaids and angels
   George Mackay Brown (1921–1996), Beachcomber

The Second Sight is an unwelcome gift. To whoever has it,
visions come not of his own seeking, and their significance
is almost invariably tragic.
   I.F. Grant (1887–1983), Highland Folk Ways

Late, late in a gloamin' when all was still,
When the fringe was red on the westlin' hill,
The wood was sere, the moon i' the wane,
The reek o' the cot hung over the plain,
Like a little wee cloud in the world its lane;
When the ingle glowed wi' an eiry leme –
Late, late in the gloaming Kilmeny came hame!
   James Hogg (1770–1835), Kilmeny

A murmuring sough is on the wood,
And the witching star is red as blood.
   James Hogg, A Witch's Chant

And underneath the wheele saw I there
An ugly pit as deep as ony hell,
That to behold thereon I quoke for fear;
Bot o thing heard I, that who there-in fell
Come no more up again tidings to tell.
   King James I (1394–1437), The Kingis Quair

Across the silent stream
Where the dream-shadows go,
From the dim blue Hill of Dream
I have heard the West Wind blow.
   Fiona MacLeod (William Sharp, 1855–1905),
   From the Hills of Dream

And, dancing on each chimney top,
I saw a thousand darling imps
Keeping time with skip and hop.
   William Bell Scott (1811–1890), The Witch's Ballad

... thru the flicherin' floichan-drift
A beast cam doun the hill.
It steppit like a stallion,
Wha's heid hauds up a horn,
And weel the men o' Scotland kent
It was the unicorn.
William Soutar (1898–1943), Birthday

For there was Janet comin' doun the clachan – her or her
likeness, nane could tell – wi' her neck thrawn, an' her heid
on ae side, like a body that has been hangit, an' a girn on
her face like an unstreakit corp.
Robert Louis Stevenson (1850–1894), Thrawn Janet

Food and Drink

O gude ale comes and gude ale goes,
Gude ale gars me sell my hose,
Sell my hose and pawn my shoon,
Gude ale hauds my heart aboon.
Anonymous

Moderation, sir, aye. Moderation is my rule. Nine or ten is
reasonable refreshment, but after that it's apt to degenerate
into drinking.
Anonymous

Not too high, not too low, not too fast, and not too slow.
*Traditional rhyme for working the 'fro' stick' to mix cream,
whey and oatmeal.*

Tatties an' pint
*Traditional phrase for a meal consisting only of potatoes.
Eaters could 'point' at fowls outside, or fish hanging to dry.*

Its fried I'm fired for:
Sober Black Pudding
on a broad bay of bacon
with an egg like a solar flare
 John Aberdein (1947–), Sabbath Breakfast

On the ferry I also have Cal Mac curry and chips with lots
of tomato sauce. This is, I realise, your basic poor/
horribilist cuisine … mass-production time-warp pseudo-
curry
 Iain Banks (1954–2013), Raw Spirit

In dinner talk it is perhaps allowable to fling any faggot
rather than let the fire go out.
 Sir J.M. Barrie (1860–1937)

I once saw an English guy in Glasgow trying to order a pint
of lager and lime and the barman went: 'We don't do
cocktails.'
 Frankie Boyle (1972–)

'Dish or no dish,' rejoined the Caledonian, 'there's a deal
o' fine confused feedin' about it, let me tell you.'
 John Brown (1810–1882), Horae Subsecivae, *on Haggis.*

Some hae meat and canna eat,
And some hae nane that want it;
But we hae meat, and we can eat,
And sae the Lord be thankit.
 'The Selkirk Grace', attributed to Robert Burns (1759–1796)

See Social-life and Glee sit down
All joyous and unthinking,
Till, quite transmogrified, they've grown
Debauchery and Drinking.
 Robert Burns, An Address to the Unco Guid

We'll tak' a richt gude-willie waught
For Auld Lang Syne.
 Robert Burns, Auld Lang Syne

Freedom an' whisky gang thegither
> *Robert Burns,* The Author's Earnest Cry and Prayer to
> the Right Honourable and Honourable, the Scotch
> Representatives in the House of Commons

Liquid madness
> *Thomas Carlyle (1795–1881),* On Chartism

Nip-pint, Nip-pint –
Mustn't-get-drunk, mustn't-get-drunk.
Nip-pint, Nip-pint –
Tae pot wi' it a', tae pot wi' it a'.
> *Robin Cockburn,* The Galliard *(1948)*

Advocaat: the alcoholic's omelette.
> *Sir Billy Connolly (1942–),* Gullible's Travels

There is no finer breakfast than flounders fried in oatmeal
with a little salt butter, as ever they came out of the water,
with their tails jerking 'flip-flop' in the frizzle of the pan.
> *S.R. Crockett (1859–1914),* The Raiders

I am not fond of devilled stoat.
> *Donald Dewar (1937–2000) (a curry enthusiast) on being
> asked if he had enjoyed a meal in a certain Indian
> restaurant*

the grossly overrated potato, that marvel of insipidity.
> *Norman Douglas (1868–1952),* Together

A double Scotch is about the size of a small Scotch before
the War, and a single Scotch is nothing more than a dirty
glass.
> *Lord Dundee (1872–1924)*

There's nothing as good as a pot of kale with an auk in it.
> *Old man from Deerness, Orkney, quoted in Alexander
> Fenton,* Scottish Country Life *(1976).* Kale: *broth;* auk:
> *guillemot.*

The cure for which there is no disease
  John Ferguson (fl. 19th century), on whisky

Whan big as burns the gutters rin,
Gin ye hae catcht a droukit skin,
To Luckie Middlemist's loup in,
And sit fu' snug
O'er oysters and a dram o' gin,
Or haddock lug
  Robert Fergusson (1750–1774), Auld Reekie

And they'd broth, it was good, and the oatcakes better; and
then boiled beef and potatoes and turnip; and then rice
pudding with prunes; and then some tea.
  Lewis Grassic Gibbon (James Leslie Mitchell, 1901–1935),
  Sunset Song

Single malts must be drunk with circumspection. Contrary
to the old joke about the Highlander liking two things to be
naked, one of them whisky, malts are best drunk with a
little water to bring out the aroma and flavour.
  Neil M. Gunn (1891–1973), Whisky and Scotland

Oh, the dreadfu' curse o' drinkin'!
Men are ill, but to my thinkin',
Lookin' through the drucken fock,
There's a Jenny for ilk Jock.
  Janet Hamilton (1795–1873), Oor Location

They drank the water clear,
Instead of wine, but yet they made good cheer.
  Robert Henryson (c.1425–c.1500),
  The Town Mouse and the Country Mouse

But he does have a packet of potato crisps which he can
stuff between two slices of margarined bread. A piece on
crisps. Aye beautiful. Crunchy and munchy. And a cup of
good strong coffee.
  James Kelman (1946–), A Disaffection

How beit we want the spices and the winis,
Or uther strange fructis delicious,
We have als gude, and more needfull for us.
  Sir David Lindsay (c.1490–1555),
  The Dreme of the Realme of Scotland

'He's dead now, but he lived to a great age. I mind him
saying once – he was fou' at the time – "Man, I've only got
one vice, but it's given me more pleasure than all my
virtues." '
  Eric Linklater (1899–1974), Magnus Merriman

Sausages is the boys!
  *Jimmy Logan (1928–2001), catch-phrase from the radio
  show 'It's All Yours'*

If it was raining, it was 'We'll have a dram to keep out the
wet'; if it was cold, 'We'll have a dram to keep out the
cold'; and if it was a fine day why then, 'We'll drink its
health.'
  J.A. MacCulloch (1868–1950), on Skye in the 19th century

… it is a thoroughly democratic dish, equally available and
equally honoured in castle, farm and croft. Finally, the use
of the paunch of the animal as the receptacle of the
ingredients gives the touch of romantic barbarism so dear
to the Scottish heart.
  F. Marian McNeill (1885–1973), The Scots Kitchen,
  on haggis

Just a wee deoch an doruis,
Just a wee drop, that's a';
Just a wee deoch an doruis,
Afore ye gang awa'.
There's a wee wifie waitin'
In a wee but-and-ben;
But if ye can say 'It's a braw bricht moonlicht nicht',
It's a' richt, ye ken.
  R.F. Morrison, sung by Sir Harry Lauder (1911)

... though we're a' fearfu' fond o' oor parritch in Scotland, and some men mak' a brag o' takin' them every mornin' just as if they were a cauld bath, we're gey gled to skip them at a holiday and just be daein' wi' ham and eggs.
Neil Munro (1863–1930), Erchie, My Droll Friend

'The honestest thing I ever saw said aboot tea was in a grocer's window in Inverness – Our Unapproachable: 2s6d.'
Neil Munro, Jimmy Swan, The Joy Traveller

Wha'll buy caller herrin'?
They're bonny fish and halesome fairin':
Wha'll buy caller herrin'
New-drawn frae the Forth?
Lady Nairne (1766–1845), Caller Herrin'

A month without an R in it has nae richt being in the year.
Christopher North (John Wilson, 1785–1854), Noctes Ambrosianae

If the good Lord had wanted us to know about cuisine, he would never have given us crispy pancakes.
Ian Pattison (1950–), The Rab C. Nesbitt Scripts (1990)

'Ach, it's sair cheenged times at Castle Grant, when gentlemans can gang to bed on their ain feet.'
Dean E.B. Ramsay (1793–1872), Reminiscences of Scottish Life and Character

Here we are, progressing tenfold, buying the right bread, real croissants, we're making fresh muesli and we understand what a great cup of coffee is. And then some idiot brings out a deep-fried chocolate sandwich.
Gordon Ramsay (1966–)

I had always an unbreakeable rule, and that was when things were looking thoroughly bad to go out to a restaurant and have a good dinner and a bottle of wine.
John M. Robertson (1856–1933), 60th birthday speech

'Lord, for what we are about to receive
Help us to be truly thankful – Aimen –
Wumman, ye've pit ingans in't again.'
    Tom Scott (1918–1995), Auld Sanct-Aundrians

And there will be fadges and brochen,
Wi' fouth o' good gabbocks o' skate,
Powsowdie, and drammock and crowdie,
An' caller nowtfeet in a plate.
An' there will be partens and buckies,
And whitin's and speldin's enew,
And singit sheep's heid, and a haggis,
And scadlips to sup till ye spue.
    Attributed to Francis Sempill (c.1616–1682),
    The Wedding of Maggie and Jock

Tattie-scones, and the mealy-dot,
And a whack o' crumpy-crowdie;
And aye a bit pickle in the pat
For onie orra body.
    William Soutar (1898–1943), Hamely Fare

Human Nature

Friends are lost by calling often; and by calling seldom.
    Anonymous

And muckle thocht our gudewife to hersell,
But never a word she spak.
    Anonymous, Get Up and Bar the Door

It's pride puts a' the country doun,
Sae tak' your auld cloak about ye.
    Anonymous, Tak' Your Auld Cloak About Ye

For much better it is
To bide a friend's anger than a foe's kiss.
Alexander Barclay (c.1475–1552),
The Mirrour of Good Manners

I have everything here to make me happy except the faculty
of being happy.
Jane Welsh Carlyle (1801–1866), Letters

The greatest of faults, I should say, is to be conscious of
none.
Thomas Carlyle (1795–1881), On Heroes, Hero-Worship,
and the Heroic in History

In all times and places the Hero has been worshipped. It
will ever be so. We all love great men.
Thomas Carlyle, On Heroes, Hero-Worship, and the
Heroic in History

We have not the love of greatness, but the love of the love
of greatness.
Thomas Carlyle, Essays

To find a friend one must close one eye. To keep him – two.
Norman Douglas (1868–1952), Almanac

It is the restriction placed on vice by our social code which
makes its pursuit so peculiarly agreeable.
Kenneth Grahame (1859–1932)

It is not contrary to reason to prefer the destruction of the
whole world to the scratching of my finger.
David Hume (1711–1776),
A Treatise Upon Human Nature

Here am I, who have written on all sorts of subjects
calculated to arouse hostility, moral, political, and religious;
and yet I have no enemies, except indeed, all the Whigs, all
the Tories, and all the Christians.
　　David Hume, quoted in Lord Brougham's Men of Letters
　　and Science in the Reign of George III

a lie so obvious it was another way
of telling the truth
　　Norman MacCaig (1910–1996), Queen of Scots

The great men sayis that their distress
Comis for the peoples wickedness;
The people sayis for the transgressioun
Of great men, and their oppressioun:
Bot nane will their awin sin confess.
　　Sir Richard Maitland (1496–1586),
　　How Suld Our Commonweill Endure

I do not know him quite so well
As he knows me.
　　Robert F. Murray (1863–1894), Adventure of a Poet

While exploring a particularly wild and uncultivated region
of Africa, Mungo Park unexpectedly came across a gibbet.
'The sight of it', he later remarked, 'gave me infinite
pleasure, as it proved that I was in a civilised society.'
　　Mungo Park (1771–1806), quoted in C. Fadiman,
　　The Little, Brown Book of Anecdotes (*1985*)

Oh, what a tangled web we weave,
When first we practice to deceive.
　　Sir Walter Scott (1771–1832), Marmion

Should auld acquaintance be forgot, and never thought
upon?
　　Francis Sempill (c.1616–1685), 'Auld Lang Syne', from
　　James Watson's Choice Collection of Scots Poems, *1711*

So long as we are loved by others I should say that we are almost indispensable; and no man is useless while he has a friend.
Robert Louis Stevenson (1850–1894)

The cruellest lies are often told in silence.
Robert Louis Stevenson (1850–1894), Virginibus Puerisque

The conscience has morbid sensibilities; it must be employed but not indulged, like the imagination or the stomach.
Robert Louis Stevenson, Ethical Studies

When I came into Scotland I knew well enough what I was to expect from my enemies, but I little foresaw what I meet with from my friends.
Prince Charles Edward Stuart (1720–1788), letter, quoted in Blaikie, Itinerary of Prince Charles Stuart (1897)

But I strode on austere;
No hope could have no fear.
James Thomson (1834–1882), The City of Dreadful Night

Lamentations

When Alysandyr our King was dede
That Scotland led in luf and le,
Away was sons of ale and brede,
Of wine and wax, of gamyn and gle;
Our gold was changyd into lead.
Christ born into Virginitie
Succour Scotland and remede
That stad is in perplexytie.
Anonymous

Ohone, alas, for I was the youngest,
And aye my weird it was the hardest.
Anonymous, Cospatrick

O there is nane in Galloway,
There's nane at a' for me.
I ne'er lo'ed a lad but ane,
And he's drooned in the sea.
Anonymous, The Lawlands o' Holland

Yestreen the Queen had four Maries,
The night she'll hae but three:
There was Marie Seton, and Marie Beaton,
And Marie Carmichael, and me.
Anonymous, The Queen's Marie

To seek het water beneith cauld ice,
Surely it is a great folie –
I have asked grace at a graceless face,
But there is nane for my men and me!
Anonymous, Johnie Armstrong

Ye Hielands and ye Lawlands, o whaur hae ye been –
They hae slain the Earl o' Moray
And laid him on the green.
Anonymous, The Bonnie Earl o' Moray. *A mishearing of
the third line when read aloud, as 'And Lady Mondegreen',
has given us the 'mondegreen' as a name for similar
instances.*

I took his body on my back,
And whiles I gaed, and whiles I sat;
I digg'd a grave, and laid him in,
And happ'd him with the sod sae green.
Anonymous, The Lament of the Border Widow

To have, to hold, and then to part
Is the great sorrow of the human heart
Inscription from St Monans Churchyard, Fife

They make a desert, and they call it peace.
*Words about the Romans, ascribed to Calgacus, Caledonian
war leader, at Mons Graupius, AD84, in Tacitus,* Agricola

Few, few shall part where many meet!
The snow shall be their winding-sheet,
And every turf beneath their feet
Shall be a soldier's sepulchre!
  Thomas Campbell (1777–1844), Hohenlinden

I've seen the smiling of Fortune beguiling,
I've felt all its favours and found its decay
  Alison Cockburn (1712–1794), The Flowers of the Forest

Quhome to sall I complene my wo,
And kyth my kairis ane or mo,
I knaw nocht amang rich nor pure
Quha is my freynd, quha is my fo;
For in the warld may none assure
  William Dunbar (c.1460–1520),
    None May Assure in This Warld

Now they are moaning on ilka green loaning,
The flowers o' the Forest are a' wede away.
  Jane Elliott (1727–1805), The Flowers o' the Forest

Now is my breist with stormy stoundis stad,
Wrappit in woe, ane wretch full of wane.
  Robert Henryson (c.1425–c.1500),
    The Testament of Cresseid

Alas! How easily things go wrong!
A sigh too deep or a kiss too long,
And then comes a mist and a weeping rain,
And life is never the same again.
  George Macdonald (1824–1905), Phantastes

No more, no more, no more for ever
In war or peace shall return MacCrimmon;
No more, no more, no more for ever
Shall love or gold bring back MacCrimmon!
Norman MacLeod (1812–1872), Cumha mhic Criomein
('MacCrimmon's Lament') to a tune of Donald Bàn
MacCrimmon (d. 1746), translated by J. S. Blackie

He fell as the moon in a storm; as the sun from the midst of
his course, when clouds rise from the waste of the waves,
when the blackness of the storm inwraps the rocks of
Ardannidir. I, like an ancient oak on Morven, I moulder
alone in my place. The blast has lopped my branches away;
and I tremble at the wings of the north. Prince of warriors,
Oscur my son! Shall I see thee no more.
James Macpherson (1736–1796),
Fragments of Ancient Poetry

In this new yeir I see but weir,
Nae cause to sing;
In this new yeir I see but weir,
Nae cause there is to sing.
Sir Richard Maitland (1496–1586), On the New Yeir 1560

Adieu for ay! This a lang gude nicht!
Alexander Montgomerie (c.1545–c.1611),
A Lang Gude Nicht

That year we thatched the house with snowflakes
Derick Thomson (1921–2012), 'Strathnaver'
(Srath Nabhair)

Landscape and Nature

Tweed says to Till
Whit gars ye rin sae still?
Till says to Tweed,
Tho' ye rin fast
And I rin slaw,
For ae man that ye droon,
I droon twa.
Traditional

Scotland the wee
Tom Buchan (1931–1995), Scotland the Wee

Nature, which is the time-vesture of God, and reveals Him
to the wise, hides Him from the foolish.
Thomas Carlyle (1795–1881), Sartor Resartus

Our fathers fought, so runs the glorious tale,
To save you, country mine, from tyrants rash,
And now their bones and you are up for sale,
The smartest bidder buys for ready cash.
J.R. Christie, My Native Land *(c.1910)*

Hame, hame, hame, hame, fain wad I be!
Hame, hame, hame, hame, to my ain countrie!
Allan Cunningham (1784–1842) Hame, Hame, Hame

… ownership is really custodianship.
Sir Frank Fraser Darling (1903–1979), Island Farm

The daisy did onbreid her crownell small,
And every flour unlappit in the dale
Gavin Douglas (1475–1522), Prologue to the Aeneid

the leaf is the chief product and phenomenon of life: this is
a green world, with animals comparatively few and small,
and all dependent on the leaves. By leaves we live.
  Sir Patrick Geddes (1854–1932), lecture in Dundee, 1927

... and a darkness down on the land he loved better than
his soul or God.
  Lewis Grassic Gibbon (James Leslie Mitchell, 1901–1935),
  Sunset Song

the land was forever, it moved and changed below you, but
was forever, you were close to it and it to you, not at a
bleak remove it held you and hurted you.
  Lewis Grassic Gibbon, Sunset Song

This is my country
The land that begat me,
These windy spaces
Are surely my own.
  Sir Alexander Gray (1882–1967), Scotland

The muirlan' burnie, purple-fringed
Wi' hinny-scented heather,
Whaur gowden king-cups blink aneath
The brecken's waving feather.
  Janet Hamilton (1795–1873), Auld Mither Scotland

There's gowd in the breast of the primrose pale,
An' siller in every blossom;
There's riches galore in the breeze of the vale,
And health in the wild wind's bosom.
  James Hogg (1770–1835), There's Gowd in the Breast

And oh! What grand's the smell ye'll get
Frae the neep-fields by the sea!
  Violet Jacob (1863–1946), The Neep Fields by the Sea

Scotland small? Our multiform, our infinite Scotland
  small?
Only as a patch of hillside may be a cliché corner
To a fool who cries 'Nothing but heather!'
  Hugh MacDiarmid (C.M. Grieve, 1892–1978),
  Scotland Small?

Let them popple, let them pirl,
Plish-plash and plunk and plop and ploot,
In quakin' quaw or fish-currie,
I ken a' they're aboot.
  Hugh MacDiarmid, Water Music

And heavy on the slumber of the moorland
The hardship and poverty of the thousands
of crofters and the lowly of the lands
  Sorley Maclean (1911–1996), The Cuillin

The curled young bracken unsheath their green claws
  Fiona MacLeod (William Sharp, 1855–1905)

Scotland is bounded on the South by England, on the East
by the rising sun, on the North by the arory-bory-Alice and
on the West by Eternity.
  Nan Shepherd (1893–1981), Quarry Wood

This is the land God gave to Andy Stewart –
  Iain Crichton Smith (1928–1998),
  The White Air of March

Anyone who aspires to being made a mummy, need only
arrange to be buried in a bog.
  Andrew Young (1885–1971), A Retrospect of Flowers

Primula Scotica might be an even better emblem for
Scotland. It is not common everywhere like the Thistle; it
is confined to Scotland, growing nowhere else.
  Andrew Young, A Retrospect of Flowers

The Law

Let them bring me prisoners, and I'll find them law.
> *Lord Braxfield (1722–1799), Tory judge of the Court of*
> *Session*

Muckle he made o' that – he was hanget.
> *Lord Braxfield, in a political trial, in reply to the plea that*
> *Jesus Christ too was a reformer, quoted by Lord Cockburn*
> *in* Memorials of His Time *(1856)*

Ye're a verra clever chiel', man, but ye'll be nane the waur
o' a hanging.
> *Lord Braxfield, to a defendant, quoted by J. G. Lockhart,*
> Memoirs of the Life of Sir Walter Scott *(1837–8)*

A fig for those by law protected!
Liberty's a glorious feast!
> *Robert Burns (1759–1796),* The Jolly Beggars

I knew a very wise man ... he believed that if a man were
permitted to make all the ballads, he need not care who
should make the laws of a nation.
> *Andrew Fletcher of Saltoun (1653–1716),* An Account of a
> Conversation Concerning a Right Regulation of
> Governments for the Common Good of Mankind

We advocates are trained to laugh at judges' jokes. It's the
way they tell them.
> *Ian Hamilton QC (1925–2022), blog, 30 September 2011*

Justice may nocht have dominatioun,
But where Peace makis habitatioun.
> *Sir David Lindsay (c.1490–1555),*
> The Dreme of the Realme of Scotland

A Judge has sentenced himself to a suicide's grave?
– The nearest to a just sentence any judge ever gave.
  Hugh MacDiarmid (C.M. Grieve, 1892–1978),
  A Judge Commits Suicide

The place commanded us by God,
where we can't travel moor or strand,
and every bit of fat or value
they have grabbed with Land Law from us.
  Mary Macpherson (1821–1898), Brosnachadh nan Gaidheal
  (Incitement of the Gaels, translated by William Neill)

Never give your reasons; for your judgement will probably
be right, but your reasons almost certainly will be wrong.
  Lord Mansfield (1705–1793), Advice to Judges

… that bastard verdict, Not proven. I hate that Caledonian
medium quid. One who is not proven guilty is innocent in
the eye of law.
  Sir Walter Scott (1771–1832), Journal, *1827*

Love

Follow love, and it will flee:
Flee it, and it follows ye.
  Anonymous

It is a pity I was not with the Black-haired Lad on the brow
of the hill under the rainstorms, in a small hollow of the
wilds or in some secret place; and I'll not take a greybeard
while you come to my mind.
  Anonymous, from Gaelic, translated by Kenneth Jackson

The white bloom of the blackthorn, she;
The small sweet raspberry blossom, she;
More fair the shy, rare glance of her eye
Than the world's wealth to me.
  From Gaelic

My heart is heich abufe,
My body is fall of bliss,
For I am set in lufe,
As weil as I wald wiss.
Anonymous, My Heart is Heich Abufe

O waly, waly! but love be bonnie
A little time, while it is new;
But when 'tis auld, it waxeth cauld,
And fades away like morning dew.
Anonymous, O Waly, Waly

Willie's rare, and Willie's fair;
And Willie's wondrous bonny:
And Willie hecht to marry me,
Gin e'er he married ony.
Anonymous, Willie's Rare

Tho' his richt e'e doth skellie, an' his left leg doth limp ill,
He's won the heart and got the hand of Kate Dalrymple.
Anonymous, Kate Dalrymple

A fine wee lass, a bonnie wee lass, is bonnie wee Jeannie
    McColl;
I gave her my mother's engagement ring and a bonnie wee
    tartan shawl.
I met her at a waddin' in the Co-operative Hall;
I wis the best man and she was the belle of the ball.
1920s music hall song popularised by Will Fyffe (c.1885–1947)

My beloved sall ha'e this he'rt tae break,
Reid, reid wine and the barley cake,
A he'rt tae break, and a mou' tae kiss,
Tho' he be nae mine, as I am his.
Marion Angus (1866–1946), Mary's Song

Gif she to my desire wad listen,
I wadna caa the king my cuisin.
J.K. Annand (1908–1993), My Weird Is Comforted

Yes, I have died for love, as others do;
But praised be God, it was in such a sort
That I revived within an hour or two.
    Sir Robert Ayton (1570–1638), On Love

But twice unhappier is he, I lairn,
That feedis in his hairt a mad desire,
And follows on a woman throw the fire,
Led by a blind and teachit by a bairn.
    Mark Alexander Boyd (1563–1601), Cupid and Venus

My luve is like a red, red rose,
That's newly sprung in June;
My luve is like a melody,
That's sweetly play'd in tune.
As fair thou art, my bonie lass,
So deep in luve am I;
And I will luve thee still, my dear,
Till a' the seas gang dry.
Till all the seas gang dry, my dear,
And the rocks melt wi' the sun,
And I will love thee still, my dear,
While the sands o' life shall run.
    Robert Burns (1759–1796), My Luve is Like a Red,
    Red Rose

My love she's but a lassie yet;
My love she's but a lassie yet:
We'll let her stand a year or twa:
She'll nae be half sae saucy yet.
    Robert Burns, My Love She's But a Lassie Yet

Her brow is like the snaw-drift,
… And dark blue is her e'e:
And for bonnie Annie Laurie
I'd lay me doun and dee.
    William Douglas (fl. c.1700), Annie Laurie

The flow'rs did smile, like those upon her face,
And as their aspen stalks those fingers band,
That she might read my case,
A hyacinth I wish'd me in her hand.
William Drummond (1585–1649), Like the Idalian Queen

So it was she knew she liked him, loved him as they said in
the soppy English books, you were shamed and a fool to
say that in Scotland.
Lewis Grassic Gibbon (James Leslie Mitchell, 1901–1935),
Sunset Song

But O, her artless smile's mair sweet,
Than hinny or than marmalete.
James Hogg (1770–1835), My Love She's But a Lassie Yet

'Oh Mary, ye're wan in a million.'
'Oh, oh, and so's yer chances.'
Hamish Imlach (1940–1996),
Cod Liver Oil and the Orange Juice

So ferre I falling into lufis dance,
That sodeynly my wit, my contenance,
My hert, my will, my nature and my mynd,
Was changit clene rycht in ane other kind.
King James I (1394–1437), The Kingis Quair

How they strut about, people in love,
How tall they grow, pleased with themselves
Jackie Kay (1961–), Late Love

'If you're goin' to speak aboot love, be dacent and and
speak aboot it in the Gaalic. But we're no talkin' aboot
love: we're talkin' aboot my merrage.'
Neil Munro (1864–1930), The Vital Spark

Ye're a bonny lad, and I'm a lassie free,
Ye're welcomer to tak' me than to let me be.
Allan Ramsay (1686–1758), The Gentle Shepherd

Love is ane fervent fire
Kendillit without desire;
Short pleasure, lang displeasure,
Repentence is the hire
    Alexander Scott (c.1520–c.1590), A Rondel of Luve

Love swells like the Solway, but ebbs like its tide.
    Sir Walter Scott (1771–1832), Lochinvar

Thy fatal shafts unerring move,
I bow before thine altar, Love.
    Tobias Smollett (1721–1771),
        The Adventures of Roderick Random

A' thru the nicht we spak nae word
Nor sinder'd bane frae bane:
A' thru the nicht I heard her hert
Gang soundin' wi' my ain.
    William Soutar (1898–1943), The Tryst

We always believe our first love is our last, and our last love
our first.
    George Whyte-Melville (1821–1878)

Men and Women

When Aberdeen and Ayr are baith ae toun,
And Tweed sall turn and rinnis into Tay ...
When Paradise is quit of heavenly hue,
She whom I luve sall steadfast be and true.
    Anonymous

I'll wager, I'll wager, I'll wager wi' you
Five hundred merks and ten,
That a maid shanna gae to the bonny broom
And a maiden return again.
    Anonymous, The Broomfield Hill

Then up sho gat ane meikle rung
And the gudeman made to the door;
Quoth he, 'Dame, I sall hauld my tongue,
For, an we fecht, I'll get the waur.'
Anonymous, The Wife of Auchtermuchty

Bell, my wife, she lo'es nae strife,
But she would guide me if she can;
And to maintain an easy life,
I aft maun yield, though I'm gudeman.
Anonymous, Tak' Your Auld Cloak About Ye

You see, dear, it is not true that woman was made from
man's rib; she was really made from his funny bone.
Sir J.M. Barrie (1860–1937), What Every Woman Knows

Ye stupid auld bitch ... I beg your pardon, mem, I mistook
ye for my wife.
Attributed to Lord Braxfield (1722–1799),
to his partner at whist

Lissy, I am looking out for a wife, and I thought you just
the person that would suit me. Let me have your answer,
aff or on, the morn, and nae mair about it.
Lord Braxfield's proposal to his second wife, recorded in
John Kay, Original Portraits *(1877)*

... our hame
Where sits our sulky, sullen dame,
Gathering her brows like gathering storm,
Nursing her wrath to keep it warm.
Robert Burns (1759–1796), Tam o' Shanter

Gin a body meet a body,
Comin' through the rye;
Gin a body kiss a body,
Need a body cry?
Ilka lassie has her laddie,
Nane, they say, ha'e I:
Yet a' the lads they smile at me,
When comin' through the rye.
    Robert Burns, Comin' Through the Rye

What is man? A foolish baby;
Vainly strives, and fights, and frets;
Demanding all, deserving nothing,
One small grave is all he gets.
    Thomas Carlyle (1795–1881), Cui Bono

There was a singular race of excellent Scotch old ladies.
They were a delightful set; strong-headed, warm-hearted
and high-spirited; the fire of their temper not always latent;
merry even in solitude; very resolute; indifferent about the
modes and habits of the modern world
    Henry Thomas Cockburn (1779–1854), Memorials

Man thinks more, woman feels more. He discovers more
but remembers less; she is more receptive and less
forgetful.
    Sir Patrick Geddes (1854–1932), The Evolution of Sex
    (with J. Arthur Thomson)

Lie over to me from the wall or else
Get up and clean the grate.
    W.S. Graham (1918–1986), Baldy Bane

... as I took a particular pleasure in the company of modest
women, I had no reason to be displeased with the reception
I got from them.
    David Hume (1711–1776), My Own Life

Says she, 'Guidmen I've kistit twa,
But a change o' deils is lichtsome, lass!'
   Violet Jacob (1863–1946), A Change o' Deils

For men were just a perfect nuisance – wasn't that so, now?
My goodness me! No wonder women always aged much
quicker than their menfolk, considering all they had to put
up with.
   Jessie Kesson (Jessie Grant Macdonald, 1916–1994),
   A Glitter of Mica

To promote a Woman to beare rule, superioritie, dominion,
or empire above any Realme, Nation or Citie, is repugnant
to Nature; contumelie to God, a thing most contrary to his
revealed will and approved ordinance; and finallie it is the
subversion of good Order, of all equitie and justice.
   John Knox (c.1513–1572) The First Blast of the Trumpet
   Against the Monstrous Regiment of Women

Oh I am wild-eyed, unkempt, hellbent, a harridan.
My sharp tongue will shrivel any man.
   Liz Lochhead (1947–), Harridan

I must say here that the race of true Scotswomen, iron
women, hardy, indomitable, humorous, gay, shrewd
women with an amazing sense of values, seems to be facing
extinction too in today's Scotland.
   Hugh MacDiarmid (C.M. Grieve, 1892–1978), Lucky
   Poet

On the one hand, you've got 'decent' men, and on the
other you've gor neanderthal misogynist bawbags – and the
middle ground is what's disappearing.
   Val McDermid (1955–)

'Buffers like you would stop the Flying Scotsman going full
tilt at Longniddry,' Binnie said. 'Fine I'd like a wee sit-out
with her.'
   Bruce Marshall (1889–1987), Teacup Terrace

For there's nae luck aboot the hoose,
There's nae luck at a';
There's little pleasure in the hoose,
When our gudeman's awa'.
W.J. Mickle (1734–1788), The Mariner's Wife

Marion, you have got a good man to be your husband, but
you will not enjoy him long: prize his company, and keep
linen by you for his winding-sheet; you will need it when
you are not looking for it, and it will be a bloody one.
*Alexander Peden (1626–1686), Covenanting minister, upon
marrying Marion Weir to John Brown in 1682*

O woman! in our hours of ease
Uncertain, coy and hard to please …
When pain and anguish wring the brow,
A ministering angel thou!
Sir Walter Scott (1771–1832), Marmion

I no great Adam and you no bright Eve
Iain Crichton Smith (1928–1998), At the Firth of Lorne

The brooding boy and sighing maid,
Wholly fain and half afraid.
Robert Louis Stevenson (1850–1894), Underwoods

I heard a phrase the other day that struck a chord with me,
'When women lift, girls rise.'
Nicola Sturgeon, (1970–), final speech to the Parliament
as First Minister, 23 March 2023

He worried about her, however; thinking that anyone who
would sleep with him would sleep with anybody.
Irvine Welsh (1957–), Trainspotting

The Mind and Medicine

Up the close and doun the stair,
But an' ben wi' Burke an' Hare.
Burke's the butcher, Hare's the thief,
Knox the boy that buys the beef.
Anonymous, 19th century, The West Port Murders

I find I'm haunted with a busie mind ...
O what a wandring thing's the Mind!
What contrares are there combin'd?
John Barclay (late 17th century)

Any really good doctor ought to be able to tell before a
patient has fairly sat down, a good deal of what is the
matter with, him or her.
Joseph Bell (1837–1911), quoted in Joseph Bell:
An Appreciation by an Old Friend *(1913)*

I am more and more persuaded that there is no complete
misery in the world that does not emanate from the bowels.
*Jane Welsh Carlyle (1801–1866), Letter to Eliza Stoddart
(1834)*

I'm schizophrenic, and so am I.
Sir Billy Connolly (1942–)

Minds are like parachutes. They only function when they
are open.
James Dewar (1842–1923), physicist (attributed)

I've never met a healthy person who worried much about
his health, or a good person who worried about his soul.
J.B.S. Haldane (1892–1964)

Herein is not only a great vanity, but a great contempt of God's good gifts, that the sweetness of men's breath, being a good gift of God, should be wilfully corrupted by this stinking smoke.

King James VI (1566–1625), A Treatise Against Tobacco

There is no seventh sense of the mystic kind … But if there is not a distinct magnetic sense, I say it is a very great wonder that there is not.

Lord Kelvin (1824–1907), presidential address to the Birmingham and Midland Institute

We are born into a world where alienation awaits us.

R.D. Laing (1927–1989), The Politics of Experience

I think for my part one-half of the nation is mad – and the other not very sound.

Tobias Smollett (1721–1771), The Adventures of Sir Launcelot Greaves

Sic a hoast hae I got:
Sic a hoast hae I got:
I dout my days are on the trot

William Soutar (1898–1943), Sic a Hoast

Ah'm no sick yet, but it's in the fuckin post, that's fir sure.

Irvine Welsh (1957–), Trainspotting

Mountains and Climbers

Any fool can climb good rock, but it takes craft and cunning to get up vegetatious schist and granite.

J.H.B. Bell, quoted in W.H. Murray, Mountaineering in Scotland

By the time you have topped a hundred Munros (the incurable stage usually), you will know Scotland – and yourself – in a fuller, richer way.

Hamish Brown (1934–), 'The Munros: A Personal View', in D. Bennet, The Munros (1985)

When he some heaps of hills hath overwent,
Begins to think on rest, his journey spent,
Till, mounting some tall mountain he do find
More heights before him than he left behind.

William Drummond (1585–1649), Flowers of Sion

There is hardly any bad luck in the mountains, only good.

Gwen Moffat (1924–), Two Star Red

Ben Nevis looms the laird of a'

Charles Murray (1864–1941), Bennachie

A mystic twilight, like that of an old chapel at vespers, pervaded these highest slopes of Buachaille ... But that was not all: a strange and powerful feeling that something as yet unknown was also within my grasp, was trembling into vision.

W.H. Murray (1913–1996), Mountaineering in Scotland

The rock is like porridge – in consistency though not quality, for porridge is part of our national heritage and a feast fit for a king. This was not.

Tom Patey (1932–1970), One Man's Mountains

'The Hielan' hills, the Hielan' hills – I never see them but they gar me grew.'

Sir Walter Scott (1771–1832), Rob Roy

All are aspects of one entity, the living mountain. The disintegrating rock, the nurturing rain, the quickening sun, the seed, the root, the bird – all are one. Eagle and alpine veronica are part of the mountain's wholeness.

Nan Shepherd (1893–1981), The Living Mountain

Above all was Suilven, throwing its dark shadow, a
mountain huger than itself.
  Andrew Young (1885–1971), A Retrospect of Flowers

Music, Dance and Song

O sing to me the auld Scotch sangs
In the braid Scottish tongue,
The sangs my father loved to hear,
The sangs my mother sung.
  Traditional, The Auld Scotch Sangs

I asked the piper 'How long does it take to learn to play a
pibroch?' He answered 'It takes seven years to learn to play
the pipes, and seven years to learn to play a pibroch. And
then you need the poetry.'
  *George Bruce (1909–2002), radio interview with Pipe Major
  Robert U. Brown, from* The Land Out There

I couldn't talk to people face to face, so I got on stage and
started screaming and squealing and twitching.
  David Byrne (1952–), Scottish-born US musician

When I have talked for a hour I feel lousy –
Not so when I have danced for a hour,
The dancers inherit the party.
  Ian Hamilton Finlay (1925–1996),
  The Dancers Inherit the Party

I have heard the story that MacCrimmon would write
down a tune on the wet sand as the tide began to ebb, and
would expect his pupils to be able to play it before the flood
tide once more flowed over the sand and washed away the
marks.
  Seton Gordon (1886–1977), A Highland Year

one thing he had learned this afternoon:
playing the pipes was not a substitute for sex!
   James Kelman (1946–), A Disaffection

I will nae priest for me shall sing,
Nor yet nae bells for me to ring,
But ae Bag-pipe to play a spring.
   Walter Kennedy (1460–1500)

Composers have to be schooled in a deep-seated tradition
and learn skills that go back not just generations but
centuries.
   Sir James MacMillan (1959–), in the National Review,
   2019

… there's an umbilical link between silence and music. It's
in the silence of our own thoughts and feelings that music
germinates.
   Sir James MacMillan, in the National Review, *2019*

I'm a piper to my trade,
My name is Rob the Ranter:
The lassies loup as they were daft,
When I blaw up my chanter.
   Francis Sempill (c.1616–1682), Maggie Lauder

… d fidl
wee aa dat soonds
still laukit insyd
waitin
fur a tym
whin im aibl
to pirswaid
dm oot.
   Mark Ryan Smith, a meideetashun upu lairnin d fidl,
   Scottish Corpus of Texts & Speech, 953

The important thing is what happens at the moment of performance, for the people who make the effort to be there: it lives with them.
Judith Weir (1954–)

I'm sick to death of people saying we've made eleven albums that all sound exactly the same. In fact we've made twelve albums that all sound exactly the same.
Angus Young (1959–), rock musician

The People

Saint Peter said to God, in ane sport word –
'Can ye nocht mak a Hielandman of this horse turd?'
God turned owre the horse turd with his pykit staff,
And up start a Hielandman as black as ony draff.
Anonymous, How the First Hielandman was Made

Nowhere beats the heart so kindly
As beneath the tartan plaid.
W.E. Aytoun (1818–1865); Charles Edward at Versailles

As Dr Johnson never said, Is there any Scotsman without charm?
Sir J.M. Barrie (1860–1937), address to Edinburgh University

The truth is that we are at bottom the most sentimental and emotional people on earth.
John Buchan (1875–1940), The Scots Tongue

From scenes like these, old Scotia's grandeur springs,
That makes her lov'd at home, rever'd abroad:
Princes and lords are but the breath of kings:
An honest man's the noblest work o' God.
Robert Burns (1759–1796), The Cottar's Saturday Night

Argument to the Scot is a vice more attractive than whisky.
Walter Elliott (1888–1958), speech to the House of Commons, 1942

This is certainly a fine country to grow old in. I could not spare a look to the young people, so much was I engrossed in contemplating their grandmothers.
Ann Grant (1755–1838), Letters from the Mountains

One of the great delusions of Scottish society is the widespread belief that Scotland is a tolerant and welcoming community and that racism is a problem confined to England's green and unpleasant land.
John Horne, 'Racism, Sectarianism and Football in Scotland', Scottish Affairs No. 12, 1995

From a physical point of view, the Celt and the Saxon are one; whatever may be the source of their mutual antagonism, it does not lie in a difference of race.
Sir Arthur Keith (1866–1955), Nationality and Race, 1919

A glance at their history or literature ... reveals what lies under the slow accent, the respectability and the solid flesh. Under the cake lies Bonny Dundee.
James Kennaway (1928–1968), Household Ghosts

For I marvel greatlie, I you assure,
Considderand the people and the ground,
That riches suld nocht in this realm redound.
Sir David Lindsay (c.1490–1555),
The Dreme of the Realme of Scotland

'We arra peepul', is the strange, defiant cry heard from some of Scotland's football terraces in the late twentieth century. But which people? A foreign visitor might well be confused.
Michael Lynch, Scotland, A New History (1991)

... a' the dour provincial thocht
That merks the Scottish breed
    Hugh MacDiarmid (C.M. Grieve, 1892–1978),
    A Drunk Man Looks at the Thistle

their lot was the lot of all poor people,
hardship, want and injury,
ever since the humble of every land
were deceived by ruling class, State and Civil Law,
and by every prostitute
who sold their soul for that price
that the bitches of the world have earned
    Sorley Maclean (1911–1996), The Cuillin

Our fathers all were poor,
Poorer our fathers' fathers;
Beyond, we dare not look.
    Edwin Muir (1887–1959), The Fathers

The Scots have always been an unhappy people; their
history is a varying record of heroism, treachery, persistent
bloodshed, perpetual feuds, and long-winded and sanguine
arguments.
    Edwin Muir, Scottish Journey

In all companies it gives me pleasure to declare that the
English, as a people, are very little inferior to the Scots.
    Christopher North (John Wilson, 1785–1854),
    Noctes Ambrosianae

For the Lord has pity on the bairns
Wha belang to Caledonie.
Her likely lads are wurlin weans
And cudna be onie ither,
Sin a toom howe is in the breist
O' their sair forjaskit mither.
    William Soutar (1898–1943), Second Childhood

The stamp-peyin self-employed ur truly the lowest form ay
vermin oan god's earth.
    Irvine Welsh (1957–), Trainspotting

Politics and Protest

All political parties die at last of swallowing their own lies.
    John Arbuthnot (1667–1735), quoted in R. Garnett,
    Life of Emerson (1988)

'A millionaire communist?'
'Why not? You've got penniless capitalists.'
'What'll happen to him when the Revolution comes?'
'He'll be commissar for Scotland, and you'll be sent to the
salt mines of Ross and Cromarty.'
    Chaim Bermant (1929–1998), Jericho Sleep Alone

I want to lead a Government humble enough to know its
place.
    *Gordon Brown (1951–), on standing for the Labour Party
    leadership, May 2007*

Class-conscious we are, and class-conscious will be
Till our fit's on the neck o' the boor-joysie
    *Socialist hymn quoted or parodied by John Buchan
    (1875–1940), in* Huntingtower

Cynicism, together with unrealistic expectation, are the two
great bugbears of politics.
    Donald Dewar (1937–2000)

Distrust of authority should be the first civic duty.
    Norman Douglas (1868–1952), An Almanac

Socialism? These days? There's the tree that never grew.
Och, a shower of shites. There's the bird that never flew.
    Carol Ann Duffy (1955–), Politico

'The late Oliver Brown ... put it well. He said that when I won Hamilton, you could feel a chill along the Labour back benches, looking for a spine to run up.'
   Winnie Ewing (1933–2023), quoted in Kenneth Roy,
   Conversations in a Small Country *(1989)*

You can no more be independence lite than pregnant lite.
   Annabel Goldie (1950–), Scottish Tory leader, quoted by
   Stuart Crawford on 'Caledonian Mercury', 31 May 2011

When they get into Parliament they are at once bitten with the absurd idea that they are no longer working men, but statesmen, and they try to behave as such.
   R.B. Cunninghame Graham (1852–1936), on his fellow
   Labour MPs, letter to Wilfrid Blunt, 1908

The Scottish Tories are an extreme case of necrophilia.
   Christopher Harvie (1944–), Cultural Weapons

A good nationalist must first of all be a good internationalist.
   Hamish Henderson (1919–2002), quoted in Timothy Neat,
   Hamish Henderson: A Biography *(2009)*

A regard for liberty, though a laudable passion, ought commonly to be subordinate to a reverence for established government.
   David Hume (1711–1776), Essays Moral and Political

I will govern according to the common weal, but not according to the common will.
   King James VI, Reply to the House of Commons, 1621

Were it no for the workin man what wad the rich man be? What care some gentry if they're weel though a' the puir wad dee?
   Ellen Johnston (c.1835–c.1874), The Last Sark

Dissolve the halo of divinity that surrounds the hereditary
title; let the people clearly understand that our present
House of Lords is composed largely of descendants of
successful pirates and rogues; do these things and you
shatter the Romance that keeps the nation numb and
spellbound while privilege picks its pockets.
Tom Johnston (1881–1965) Our Scots Noble Families

It's quite remarkable really the different ways whereby the
state requires its artists to suck dummytits.
*James Kelman (1946–), lecture to the Glasgow School of
Art, 1996*

Ah! splendid Vision, golden time,
An end of hunger, cold and crime.
An end of Rent, and end of Rank,
An end of balance at the Bank,
An end of everything that's meant
To bring Investors five per cent.
Andrew Lang (1844–1912), The New Millennium

I must follow them. I am their leader.
Andrew Bonar Law (1858–1923), quoted in E. Raymond,
Mr Balfour *(1920)*

All government is a monopoly of violence
Hugh MacDiarmid (C.M. Grieve, 1892–1978),
The Glass of Pure Water

… if I had my way
I would melt your gold payment,
pour it into your skull,
till it reached to your boots.
Iain Lòm Macdonald (c.1620–c.1707), Oran an Aghaidh
an Aonaidh (*Song Against the Union*), *citing the alleged
bribe-takers*

The Commons, faithful to their system, remained in a wise and masterly inactivity.

Sir James Mackintosh (1765–1832), Vindiciae Gallicae

Scottish separation is part of England's imperial disintegration.

John Maclean (1879–1923), Election Address, 1922

some, by no means all, organisations appear to have lost sight of the basic fact that public services are the people's services and that providers exist to deliver these on behalf of the public. The public are more than just customers of public authorities – they are owners, shareholders and stakeholders rolled into one.

Jim Martin, Scottish Ombudsman, quoted in Holyrood, *17 October 2011*

Toryism is an innate principle o' human nature – Whiggism but an evil habit.

Christopher North (John Wilson, 1785–1854), Noctes Ambrosianae

By the time the civil service has finished drafting a document to give effect to a principle, there may be little of the principle left.

Lord Reith (1889–1971), Into the Wind

What is the matter though we all fall? The cause shall not fall.

James Renwick (1662–1688), letter to his fellow-Covenanters, 1683

You suddenly realise you're no longer in government when you get into the back of your car and it doesn't go anywhere.

Sir Malcolm Rifkind (1946–), Tory politician

I believe passionately in English independence.

Alex Salmond, on BBC Newsnight, 10 January 2007

I think the English are well capable of self-government and
should be given the opportunity.
  Alex Salmond (1954–), on BBC Newsnight, 10 January
  2007

It is lawful to prevent the murder of ourselves or our
brethren, when no other way is left, by killing the
murderers before they accomplish their wicked design, if
they be habitually prosecuting it ... It is lawful – to kill
Tories or open murderers, as devouring beasts.
  Alexander Shields (c.1660–1700), A Hind Let Loose,
  Cameronian tract

Glasgow doesnae accept this; if you come tae Glasgow
we'll set about ye.
  *John Smeaton (1976–), police officer who helped to frustrate
  a terrorist attack at Glasgow Airport, quoted in* Time
  Magazine, *11 July 2007*

A'body kens oor nationalism
Is yet a thing o' sect and schism
  William Soutar (1898–1943), Vision

It is one of the little-known facts about modern Scottish
politics that it is not quite as cut-throat as people think it is.
  Nicola Sturgeon *(1970–), former First Minister*

Religion and Belief

A cold church,
A thin wretched cleric;
The body in subjection shedding tears:
Great their reward in the eyes of the King of Heaven.
  *Anonymous, 12th century verse from Gaelic, quoted in
  Hugh Cheape and I.F. Grant, 'Periods in Highland
  History' (1987), from Donald MacKinnon,* A Descriptive
  Catalogue of Gaelic Manuscripts *(1912)*

Lufe God abufe al, and yi nychtbour as yi self
> *Inscription on 'John Knox's House', High Street,*
> *Edinburgh (16th century)*

Better keep the devil out, than have to put him out.
> *Anonymous*

Elspeth Buchan: Come and toil in the garden of the Lord!
Old man: Thank ye, but He wasna ower kind to the first
gairdner that he had.
> *Apocryphal anecdote of 'The Woman of Revelation'*
> *(1738–1791)*

O Lord! Thou art like a mouse in a drystane dyke, aye
keekin' out at us frae holes and crannies, but we canna see
Thee.
> *Anonymous Western minister, quoted in Charles Mackay,*
> *'Poetry and Humour of the Scottish Language' (1882), from*
> *Rogers'* Illustrations of Scottish Life

'We thank thee, O Lord, for all Thy mercies; such as they
are.'
> *Anonymous Aberdeen minister, quoted in William Power,*
> Scotland and the Scots *(1934)*

Nothing to pay,
No, nothing to pay ...
Coatbridge to Glory,
And nothing to pay.
> *Baptist hymn, quoted by David Donaldson, in 'Coatbridge*
> *to Glory', from A. Kamm and A. Lean,* A Scottish
> Childhood *(1985)*

I thought God was actually floating somewhere overhead, a
stern man with a beard, something like Papa only of
enormous dimension, infinitely powerful and fearsome. Fear
indeed hung over me like a dark cloud in my childhood.
> *John Logie Baird (1888–1946),*
> Sermons, Soap and Television

If there is no future life, this world is a bad joke. But whose joke?

A.J. Balfour (1848–1930), Attributed death-bed remark

Religion fails if it cannot speak to men as they are.

William Barclay (1907–1978)

Man's extremity is God's opportunity

Lord Belhaven (1656–1708), Speech to the Scottish Parliament, 1706

Creationists have often made me doubt evolution, but probably not in the way they think.

Frankie Boyle (1972–)

An atheist is a man with no invisible means of support.

John Buchan (1875–1940), quoted in H.E. Fosdick,
On Being a Real Person

But Lord, remember me and mine
Wi' mercies temporal and divine,
That I for grace and gear may shine
Excelled by none:
And all the glory shall be thine,
Amen! Amen!

Robert Burns (1759–1796), Holy Willie's Prayer

The Church of Scotland has been high in her time, fair as the moon, clear as the sun, and terrible as an army with banners. The day has been when Zion was stately in Scotland. The terror of the Church of Scotland once took hold of all the kings and great men that passed by ... our Lord is to set up a standard, and oh! that it may be carried to Scotland. When it is set up it shall be carried through the nations, and it shall go to Rome, and the gates of Rome shall be burned with fire ...

Richard Cameron (1648–1680), Covenanting leader, his last sermon

I fear I have nothing original in me. Excepting original sin.
    Thomas Campbell (1777–1844)

The Lord knows I go up this ladder with less fear and
perturbation of spirit than ever I entered the pulpit to preach.
    *Donald Cargill (1619–1681), Covenanter minister, at his
    execution*

Man's unhappiness, as I construe, comes of his Greatness,
it is because there is an Infinite in him, which with all his
cunning he cannot quite bury under the Finite.
    Thomas Carlyle (1795–1881)

For me as an individual the worst thing in this unhappy age
in which I have grown old is that one was born into a faith
which could not, without deceit or strain, be maintained.
    Catherine Carswell (1879–1946), Lying Awake

Then the folk were sair pitten aboot,
An' they cried, as the weather grew waur:
'Oh Lord! We ken we hae sinn'd,
But a joke can be carried owre far!'
Then they chapped at the ark's muckle door,
To speir gin douce Noah had room;
But Noah never heedit their cries;
He said, 'This'll learn ye to soom.'
    W.D. Cocker (1882–1970), The Deluge (*Of the same
    occasion comes 'Weel, ye ken noo': God's response to the
    sinners who cried, 'Lord, Lord, we didna ken!'*)

The wark gangs bonnily on.
    *Attributed to David Dickson (c.1583–1663) in Henry
    Guthry*, Memoirs of Scottish Affairs, Civil and
    Ecclesiastical (*1702*), *on executions of opponents of the
    Covenanters, 1645*

The test of Religion, the final test of Religion, is not
Religiousness but Love. Greatest thing in the world.
    Henry Drummond (1851–1897), Beautiful Thoughts

Nearly every great evil, religious, political, social and commercial, which Alba labours under owes its existence or its continuation to Protestantism.

    Ruaraidh Erskine of Mar (1869–1960), in Guth na Bliadhna (*Voice of the Time*)

The truth is, my friends, you might as weel expect to see my red coo climb the muckle pear tree in the manse garden tail first and whistle like a laverock!

    William Faichney (1805–1854), in a sermon about the rich entering the Kingdom of Heaven, quoted in Hugh MacDiarmid, Lucky Poet (*1943*)

An annibabtist is a thing I am not a member of: – I am a Pisplikan just now and a Prisbetern at Kercaldy my native town which though dirty is clein in the country.

    Marjory Fleming (1803–1811), Journals

'Villain, dost thou say mass at my lug?'

    Jenny Geddes (c.1600–1660), to the Dean of St Giles, on the first use of the Book of Common Prayer, *23 July 1637*

I confess that, as an impartial outsider, I hope that as long as there are an appreciable number of Protestants, they will be balanced by some Catholics; for, while both bodies have been about equally hostile to truth, the Catholics have on the whole been kinder to beauty.

    J.B.S. Haldane (1892–1964), Science and Ethics

Nothing in the world delights a truly religious people so much as consigning them to eternal damnation.

    James Hogg (1770–1835), The Private Memoirs and Confessions of a Justified Sinner

Upon the whole, we may conclude, that the Christian Religion not only was at first attended by miracles, but even to this day cannot be believed by any reasonable person without one.

    David Hume (1711–1776), An Enquiry Concerning Human Understanding

What strange objects of adoration are cats and monkies?
says the learned doctor. They are a least as good as the
relics or rotten bones of martyrs
  David Hume, The Natural History of Religion

revelation when it condescended to describe the manner of
man's creation went sadly astray.
  Sir Arthur Keith (1866–1955), Evolution and Ethics

Do not be afraid of being free-thinkers. If you think
strongly enough you will be forced by science to the belief
in God, which is the foundation of all Religion. You will
find science not antagonistic, but helpful to Religion.
  Lord Kelvin (1824–1907), Address to the Rev. Professor
  Henslow, London, 1903

It was only later I came to the conclusion that Eve had
been framed.
  Helena Kennedy (1950–), Eve Was Framed: Women and
  British Justice

A man with God is always in the majority
  *Attributed to John Knox (c.1513–1572); quoted also as
  'God and one are always a majority' by Mary Slessor, in
  James Buchan*, The Expendable Mary Slessor (1980)

Seeing that impossible it is, but that either I shall offend
God or else that I shall displease the world, I have
determined to obey God, notwithstanding that the world
shall rage thereat.
  John Knox (c.1513–1572)

... the reik of Maister Patrik Hammyltoun hes infected as
many as it blew upoun.
  John Lyndsay (fl. 16th century), Letter to Archbishop
  Beaton on the burning of Patrick Hamilton, 1528, quoted in
  John Knox, History of the Reformation in Scotland

Change and decay in all around I see
   Henry Francis Lyte (1793–1847), Abide With Me

Let men find the faith that builds mountains
Before they seek the faith that moves them.
   Hugh MacDiarmid, (C.M. Grieve, 1892–1978),
   On a Raised Beach

The principal part of faith is patience
   George Macdonald (1824–1905)

Love of our neighbour is the only door out of the dungeon
of self.
   George Macdonald

Courage, brother! do not stumble
Though the path be dark as night
There's a star to guide the humble,
Trust in God, and do the right.
   Norman Macleod (1812–1872), Trust in God

Make me a captive, Lord,
And then I shall be free
   George Matheson (1842–1906), Make Me a Captive, Lord

The Reformation was a kind of spiritual strychnine of
which Scotland took an overdose.
   Willa Muir (1890–1970), Mrs Grundy in Scotland

The gude auld Kirk o' Scotland,
She's nae in ruins yet!
   George Murray (1819–1868), The Auld Kirk o' Scotland

A young girl sat upon the cutty-stool at St Andrews … was
asked who was the father of her child? How can I tell, she
replied artlessly, amang a wheen o' Divinity students?
   Dean E.B. Ramsay (1793–1872),
   Reminiscences of Scottish Life and Character

Being in a minister's house, there was the minimum of religious consolation.
John Macnair Reid (1895–1954), Homeward Journey

in large measure a compilation of simple Semitic myth and tradition, forged priestly codes, fabulous and falsified history, and books written by anybody other than those whose names they bear: its cosmology is in the terms of the case mere barbaric fantasy, and its ethic frequently odious.
John M. Robertson (1856–1933), Explorations, *on the Bible*

Suffering is the professor's golden garment.
Samuel Rutherford (c.1600–1661), Letter to Marion McNaught, 1637

No man can be an unbeliever nowadays. The Christian apologists have left one nothing to disbelieve.
Saki (H.H. Munro, 1870–1916)

I've read the secret name o' Knox's God.
The gowd calf 'Getting On'
Tom Scott (1918–1995), Fergus

The god can no more exist without his people than the nation without its god.
William Robertson Smith (1846–1894),
The Religion of the Semites

Nothing has afforded me so convincing a proof of the unity of the Deity as these purely mental conceptions of numerical and mathematical science which have been by slow degrees vouchsafed to man, and are still granted in these latter times by the Differential Calculus, now superseded by the Higher Algebra, all of which must have existed in that sublimely omniscient Mind from eternity.
Mary Somerville (1780–1872), Personal Recollections

Nae schauchlin' testimony here –
We were a' damned, an' that was clear.
I owned, wi' gratitude an' wonder,
He was a pleisure to sit under.
   Robert Louis Stevenson (1850–1894),
   The Scotsman's Return from Abroad

whosoever will not seek the Lord God of Israel shall be put
to death, whether small or great, whether Man or woman
   Sir James Stewart (1645–1713), Ius Populi Vindicatum
   (1669), proposal for a new Covenant

You can't endure an hour of their society here, and they
pester you to come and spend eternity with them!
   James Thomson (1834–1882), Principal Tulloch on
   Personal Immortality, *on converters*

That snod faith's gone, but the steeple aye thrists frae the
hairt o the toon
   Raymond Vettese (1950–), The Richt Noise

The Eleventh Commandment: Thou shalt not be found
out.
   George Whyte-Melville (1821–1878)

There is a happy land,
Far, far away,
Where saints in glory stand,
Bright, bright as day.
   Andrew Young (1807–1889)

There is a happy land
Down in Duke Street Jail,
Where all the prisoners stand
Tied to a nail.
   Children's burlesque of the preceding item

Science and the Scientific Approach

Science is of no party.
  A.J. Balfour (1848–1930), Politics and Political Economy

The scientific man is the only person who has anything
new to say and who does not know how to say it.
  Sir J.M. Barrie (1860–1937)

The only machine I ever understood was a wheelbarrow,
and that imperfectly.
  E.T. Bell (1883–1960), Scottish-born US mathematician

'Obvious' is the most dangerous word in mathematics.
  E.T. Bell

Millions, millions – did I say millions?
Billions and trillions are more like the fact.
Millions, billions, trillions, quadrillions,
Make the long sum of creation exact,
  J.S. Blackie (1809–1895), 'Song of Geology', quoted in
  C.P. Finlayson, 'The Symposium Academicum', in
  G. Donaldson, Four Centuries: Edinburgh University
  Life *(1983)*

He devoured every kind of learning. Not content with
chemistry and natural philosophy, he studied anatomy, and
was one day found carrying home for dissection the head of
a child that had died of some hidden disorder.
  Lord Brougham (1778–1868), Lives of Men of Literature
  and Science in the Age of George III, *on James Watt*
  (1736–1819)

A trend is a trend is a trend,
But the question is, will it bend?
Will it alter its course
Through some unforeseen force
And come to a premature end?

Sir Alexander Cairncross (1911–1998), 'Stein Age
Forecaster', in Economic Journal, *1969*

The citizen is told that ignorance of the law is no excuse;
ignorance of science should not be either.

Ritchie Calder (1906–1982), Science Profiles

He ever loved the Mathematics, because he said even God
Almighty works by geometry.

S.R. Crockett (1859–1914), The Raiders

'How often have I said to you that when you have
eliminated the impossible, whatever remains, however
improbable, must be the truth?'

Sir Arthur Conan Doyle (1859–1930), The Sign of Four

It is the lone worker who makes the first advance in a
subject: the details may be worked out by a team, but the
prime idea is due to the enterprise, thought and perception
of an individual.

Sir Alexander Fleming (1881–1955), Rectorial Address to
Edinburgh University, 1951

The Creator, if he exists, has a specific preference for
beetles.

J.B.S. Haldane (1892–1964), Lecture, April 1951

No testimony is sufficient to establish a miracle, unless the
testimony be of such a kind that its falsehood would be
more miraculous than the fact which it endeavours to
establish.

David Hume (1711–1776), An Enquiry Concerning
Human Understanding

A bag of gravel is a history to me, and ... will tell wondrous tales ... mind, a bag of gravel is worth a bag of gold.
  James Hutton (1726–1797)

... when you can measure what you are speaking about, and express it in numbers, you know something about it.
  Lord Kelvin (1824–1907), lecture to the Institution of Civil Engineers (1883)

When I say a few million, I must say at the same time, that I consider a hundred millions as being a few.
  Lord Kelvin, On Geological Time

Like any other martyr of science, I must expect to be thought importunate, tedious, and a fellow of one idea, and that idea wrong. To resent this would show great want of humour, and a plentiful lack of knowledge of human nature.
  Andrew Lang (1844–1912), Magic and Religion

He clings to statistics as a drunken man clings to a lamp-post; for support rather than illumination.
  Attributed to Andrew Lang, perhaps in conversation

The thing you cannot get a pigeon-hole for is the finger-post showing the way to discovery.
  Sir Patrick Manson (1844–1922), quoted in Philip Manson-Bahr, Patrick Manson (1962)

Gin a body meet a body
Flyin' through the air,
Gin a body hit a body,
Will it fly? and where?
Ilka impact has its measure,
Ne'er an ane hae I,
Yet a' the lads they measure me,
Or, at least, they try.
  James Clerk Maxwell (1831–1879), In Memory of Edward Wilson: Rigid Body (Sings)

In fact, whenever energy is transmitted from one body to another in time, there must be a medium or substance in which the energy exists after it leaves one body and before it reaches the other.

James Clerk Maxwell,
Treatise of Electricity and Magnetism

No theory of evolution can be formed to account for the similarity of molecules, for evolution necessarily implies continuous change, and the molecule is incapable of growth or decay.

James Clerk Maxwell, Discourse on Molecules

During cycles long anterior to the creation of the human race, and while the surface of the globe was passing from one condition to another, whole races of animals – each group adapted to the physical conditions in which they lived – were successively created and exterminated.

Sir Roderick Murchison (1792–1871), The Silurian System

Dr Black dreaded nothing so much as error and Dr Hutton dreaded nothing so much as ignorance; the one was always afraid of going beyond the truth and the other of not reaching it.

John Playfair (1748–1819), 'Life of Dr Hutton', in Transactions of the Royal Society of Edinburgh, *on Joseph Black and James Hutton*

Science is the Differential Calculus of the mind, Art the Integral Calculus; they may be beautiful when apart, but are greatest only when combined.

Sir Ronald Ross (1857–1932), quoted in Complete Poems of Hugh MacDiarmid, vol 2

I had the chloroform for several days in the house before trying it … The first night we took it Dr Duncan, Dr Keith and I all tried it simultaneously, and were all 'under the table' in a minute or two.

Sir James Young Simpson (1811–1870), Letter to Mr Waldie, November 1847

Science is the great antidote to the poison of enthusiasms and superstition.

Adam Smith (1723–1790), The Wealth of Nations

For the harmony of the world is made manifest in Form and Number, and the heart and soul and all the poetry of Natural Philosophy are embodied in the concept of mathematical beauty.

Sir D'Arcy Wentworth Thompson (1860–1948),
Growth and Form *(edition of 1942)*

The idea came into my mind, that as steam was an elastic body, it would rush into a vacuum, and if a communication was made between the cylinder and and an exhausted vessel, it would rush into it, and might there be condensed without cooling the cylinder.

James Watt (1736–1819), quoted in H.W. Dickinson,
James Watt, Craftsman and Engineer *(1935)*

The Sea and Seafaring

The waves have some mercy, but the rocks have no mercy at all.

Gaelic Proverb

In the bay the waves pursued their indifferent dances.

George Mackay Brown (1921–1996), A Winter Bride

The boats drove furrows homeward, like ploughmen
In blizzards of gulls.

George Mackay Brown, Hamnavoe

A wet sheet and a flowing sea,
A wind that follows fast,
And fills the white and rustling sail,
And bends the gallant mast.

Allan Cunningham (1791–1839),
A Wet Sheet and a Flowing Sea

O weel may the boatie row,
That fills a heavy creel,
And cleads us a' frae head to feet,
And buys our parritch meal.
    John Ewen (1741–1821), O Weel May the Boatie Row

They forgot all about the ship; they forgot everything,
except the herrings, the lithe silver fish, the swift flashing
ones, hundreds and thousands of them, the silver darlings.
    Neil Gunn (1891–1973), The Silver Darlings

In and out of the bay hesitates the Atlantic
    Norman MacCaig (1910–1996), Neglected Graveyard,
    Luskentyre

The sea-shell wants to whisper to you.
    George Macdonald (1824–1905), Summer Song

The tide was dark and heavy with the burthen that it bore.
I heard it talkin', whisperin', upon the weedy shore.
    Fiona MacLeod (William Sharp, 1855–1905),
    The Burthen of the Tide

Blue deep Barra waves are calling;
Sore sea-longing in my heart.
    Kenneth MacLeod (1871–1955), Sea-Longing

Perhaps other seas have voices for other folk, but the
western sea alone can speak in the Gaelic tongue and reach
the Gaelic heart.
    Kenneth MacLeod, Introduction to Marjory Kennedy-
    Fraser, Songs of the Hebrides

No pipes or drum to cheer them on
When siccar work to do:
'Tis the music of the tempest's song
Leads on the lifeboat crew.
    R. Robertson, The Aith Hope Lifeboat Crew (*1899*)

It's no fish ye're buying: it's men's lives.
Sir Walter Scott (1771–1832), *The Antiquary*

vague wishless seaweed floating on a tide
Iain Crichton Smith (1928–1998), Old Woman

… my kinsmen and my countrymen,
Who early and late in the windy ocean toiled
To plant a star for seamen
Robert Louis Stevenson (1850–1894), Skerryvore,
on the lighthouse-builders

Seasons and Weather

'I will go tomorrow,' said the king.
'You will wait for me,' said the wind.
Gaelic Proverb

Be it wind, be it weet, be it hail, be it sleet,
Our ship maun sail the faem
Anonymous, Sir Patrick Spens

And gurly grew the sea.
Anonymous, Sir Patrick Spens

It's dowie in the hint o' hairst,
At the wa-gang o' the swallow,
When the win' grows cauld, and the burns grow bauld,
And the wuds are hingin' yellow.
Hew Ainslie (1792–1877), The Hint o' Hairst

And saftly, saftly, ower the hill,
Comes the sma', sma' rain.
Marion Angus (1866–1946), The Lilt

Gurly grey as dragons braith
Like a ghaistie fae the grun
Cauldly, cauldly lifts the Mist
Tellin winter has begun
> *Sheena Blackhall (1947–),* Tellin the Beads o Mornin,
> Balquhidder

'Thu'll be shoors, lang-tailed shoors, an' rain a' 'tween, an'
it'll ettle tae plump; but thu'll no be a wacht o' weet.'
> *Border farmer's weather forecast, quoted by J. Brown in*
> *W. Knight,* Some Nineteenth-Century Scotsmen *(1903)*

In the north, on a showery day, you can see the rain, its
lovely behaviour over an island – while you stand a mile off
in a patch of sun
> *George Mackay Brown (1921–1996),* An Orkney Tapestry

And weary winter comin' fast
> *Robert Burns (1759–1796)* To a Mouse

With cranreuch cantie on the pane,
snaw drops sweetly, heaven-sent.
Winter's warmth is here again
and barefoot summer's lang ahint!
> *Donald Campbell (1940–2019),* Winter Bairns

There are two seasons in Scotland: June and winter.
> *Sir Billy Connolly (1942–)*

Is there any light quite like the June sun of the North and
West? It takes trouble out of the world.
> *Sir Frank Fraser Darling (1903–1979),* Island Days

The licht begouth to quinkle out and fail,
The day to darken, decline and devaill ...
Up goes the bat, with her pelit leathern flycht,
The lark descendis from the skyis hycht
Singand her complin song efter her guise.
    Gavin Douglas (1475–1522), Prologue to the Aeneid,
    on a June Evening

In to thir dark and drublie dayis
Whone sabill all the Hevin arrayis,
With mystie vapouris, cluddis and skyis,
Nature all curage me denyis
    William Dunbar (c.1460–c.1520), Meditation in Winter

Now mirk December's dowie face
Glow'rs owre the rigs wi' sour grimace
    Robert Fergusson (1750–1774), The Daft Days

The rain falling Scotchly, Scotchly
    Ian Hamilton Finlay (1925–1996), Black Tomintoul

She was a dour bitch o' a back-end, yon.
    Flora Garry, 'Ae Mair Hairst', quoted in D.K. Cameron,
    Cornkister Days *(1984)*

... the shilpit sun is thin
Like an auld man deein' slow
    Violet Jacob (1863–1946), The Rowan

... creeping over Rannoch, while the God of moorland
walks abroad with his entourage of freezing fog, his
bodyguard of snow.
    Kathleen Jamie (1962–), The Way We Live

Ah, pretty summer, e'en boast as you please;
Sweet are your gifts, but to Winter we owe
Snow on the Ochils and sun on the snow.
    Henry Johnstone (1844–1931), Winter

The world's a bear shrugged in his den.
It's snug and close in the snoring night.
And outside like chrysanthemums
The fog unfolds its bitter scent.

Norman MacCaig (1910–1996), November Night,
Edinburgh

I hear the little children of the wind
Crying solitary in lonely places.

Fiona MacLeod (William Sharp, 1855–1905),
Little Children of the Wind

Silence is in the air:
The stars move to their places.
Silent and serene the stars move to their places.

William Soutar (1898–1943), The Children

Autumnal frosts enchant the pool
And make the cart-ruts beautiful.

Robert Louis Stevenson (1850–1894), The House Beautiful

Through the hushed air the whitening shower descends,
At first thin-wavering; till at last the flakes
Fall broad and wide and fast, dimming the day
With a continual flow.

James Thomson (1700–1748), The Seasons

And one green spear
Stabbing a dead leaf from below
Kills winter at a blow.

Andrew Young (1881–1975), Last Snow

Selves and Others
(real and imaginary)

'I'll gie thee Rozie o' the Cleugh,
I'm sure she'll please thee weel eneuch.'
'Up wi' her on the bare bane dyke,
She'll be rotten or I'll be ripe.'
    Anonymous, Hey, Wully Wine

Up wi' the souters o' Selkirk,
And down wi' the Earl of Home
    Anonymous, Up Wi' the Souters o' Selkirk

I am a very promising young man.
    Robert Adam (1728–1792), letter to his family, 1756

Jeffrey, in conversation, was like a skilful swordsman
flourishing his weapon in the air; while Mackintosh, with a
thin sharp rapier, in the middle of his evolutions, ran him
through the body.
    Sir Archibald Alison (1792–1867), on Francis Jeffrey and
    Sir James Mackintosh

Queens should be cold and wise,
And she loved little things
    Marion Angus (1866–1946), Alas! Poor Queen, *on Mary I*

… such was the wisdom and authoritie of that old, little,
crooked souldier, that all, with ane incredible sumission,
from the beginning to the end, gave over themselves to be
guided by him, as if he had been Great Solyman.
    Robert Baillie (1599–1662), Letters and Journals,
    on Alexander Leslie, Earl of Leven

Oh the gladness of her gladness when she's glad,
And the sadness of her sadness when she's sad:
But the gladness of her gladness,
And the sadness of her sadness,
Are as nothing ...
To the badness of her badness when she's bad.
   Sir J.M. Barrie (1860–1937), Rosalind

Dr Campbell, looking once into a pamphlet at a
bookseller's shop, liked it so well as to purchase it; and it
was not till he had read it halfway through that he
discovered it to be of his own composition.
   Biographica Britannia, *on the author John Campbell
   (1708–1775)*

I have some fixed principles; but my existence is chiefly
conditioned by the powers of fancy and sensation.
   James Boswell (1740–1795), Journal, *on himself*

I enjoy the comedy technique of self-deprecation – but I'm
not very good at it.
   Arnold Brown (1936–)

His behaviour under all that barbarous usage was as great
and firm to the last, looking on all that was done to him
with a noble scorn, as the fury of his enemies was black and
universally detested.
   Gilbert Burnet (1643–1715), History of His Own Time,
   on the death of Montrose

A little upright, pert, tart, tripping wight,
And still his precious self his dear delight.
   Robert Burns (1759–1796), The Poet's Progress

If you awakened him from his reverie, and made him attend to the subject of the conversation, he immediately began a harangue, and never stopped till he told you all he knew about it, and with the utmost philosophical ingenuity.

Alexander Carlyle (1722–1805), quoted in R.B. Haldane,
Adam Smith, *on Adam Smith (1723–1790)*

Let me have my own way exactly in everything, and a sunnier and pleasanter creature does not exist.

ascribed to Thomas Carlyle (1795–1881), in conversation

I like to tell people when they ask 'Are you a native born?' 'No sir, I am a Scotchman,' and I feel as proud as I am sure ever Roman did when it was their boast to say 'I am a Roman citizen'.

Andrew Carnegie (1835–1918), Autobiography

Dr Joseph Black was a striking and beautiful person; tall, very thin, and cadaverously pale; his hair carefully powdered, though there was little of it except what was collected into a long thin queue; his eyes dark, clear and large, like deep pools of pure water.

Henry Thomas Cockburn, Memorials

I never heard of him dining out, except at his relation's, Joseph Black's, where his son, Sir Adam (the friend of Scott) used to say 'It was delightful to see the two rioting over a boiled turnip'.

Henry Thomas Cockburn, Memorials, *on Adam Ferguson*

More than anything else, I'd like to be an old man with a good face, like Hitchcock or Picasso.

Sir Sean Connery (1930–2020)

He could start a party in an empty room, and he often did.

Donald Dewar (1937–2000), on John Smith, Labour Party leader (1938–1994)

'He was a great fellow my friend Will,' he rang out in that deep voice of his. 'The thumb-mark of his Maker was wet in the clay of him.'

    George Douglas (George Douglas Brown, 1869–1902),
    The House With the Green Shutters

The Wardraipper of Venus boure,
To giff a doublett he is als doure,
As it war off ane futt syd frog:
Madame, ye hev a dangerouss Dog!

    William Dunbar (c.1460–c.1520), Of James Dog,
    Kepar of the Quenis Wardrop

He is nae Dog; he is a Lam.

    William Dunbar, Of the Same James, When He Had
    Pleasit Him

I love in Isa's bed to lie
O such a joy and luxury
The botom of the bed I sleep
And with great care I myself keep
Oft I embrace her feet of lillys
But she has goton all the pillies

    Marjory Fleming (1803–1811), Journals

My mother ... who had a genius for finding leaden linings.

    Janice Galloway (1955–)

He was a man of no smeddum in discourse

    John Galt (1779–1839), The Provost

Sometimes even with the very beggars I found a jocose saying as well received as a bawbee, although naturally I dinna think I was ever what could be called a funny man, but only just as ye would say a thought ajee in that way.

    John Galt, The Provost

The 'heroic young queen' in question had the face, mind, manners and morals of a well-intentioned but hysterical poodle.

Lewis Grassic Gibbon (James Leslie Mitchell, 1901–1935), Scottish Scene, *on Queen Mary I*

She'd reddish hair, and high, skeugh nose, and a hand that skelped her way through life; and if ever a soul had seen her at rest when the dark was done and the day was come he'd died of the shock and never let on.

Lewis Grassic Gibbon, Smeddum

I am of that unfortunate class who never knew what it was to be a child in spirit. Even the memories of boyhood and young manhood are gloomy.

James Keir Hardie (1856–1915), quoted in K.O. Morgan, Keir Hardie

Of riches he keepit no proper thing,
Gave as he wan, like Alexander the king.
In times of peace, meek as a monk was he,
Whan weir approachit, the richt Ector was he.

'Blind Harry' (fl. 1490s), Wallace

Auld Ramsay Mac kissed the magic duchess and turned into a puddock.

Christopher Harvie (1944–), speech on the 75th anniversary of the Saltire Society, 16 June 2011. Ramsay Macdonald was Prime Minister, 1924, and 1929–31

Now hait, now cold, now blyth, now full of woe,
Now green as leaf, now witherit and ago.

Robert Henryson (c.1425–c.1500),
The Testament of Cresseid

'What a wonderful boy he is!' said my mother.
'I'm feared he turn out to be a conceited gowk,' said old
Barnet, the minister's man.

> *James Hogg (1770–1835)*, The Private Memoirs and
> Confessions of a Justified Sinner

A sober, discreet, virtuous, regular, quiet, good-natured
man of a bad character.

> *David Hume (1711–1776), letter to Dr Clephane, on himself*

O Knox he was a bad man
he split the Scottish mind.
The one half he made cruel
and the other half unkind.

> *Alan Jackson (1938–)*, Knox

Hardie was a collier, a journalist, an agitator who held fast
to his faiths in all the storms and tempests of an agitator's
life; an incorruptible if ever there was one.

> *Tom Johnston (1881–1965)*, Memories, *on James Keir
> Hardie*

I am a stranger, visiting myself occasionally.

> *Jackie Kay (1961–)*, That Distance Apart

I've lived hereabouts all my life (more or less) largely
waiting with infinite impatience for fame to strike without
warning ... Ever the apprentice Stoic.

> *Frank Kuppner (1951–)*, PN Review 188, *July–August 2009*

... that richt redoutit Roy,
That potent prince gentle King James the Ferde

> *Sir David Lindsay (c.1490–1555)*, The Testament of the
> Papyngo, *on James IV*

She looks like a million dollars, but she only knows a
hundred and twenty words and she's got only two ideas in
her head.

> *Eric Linklater (1899–1974)*, Juan in America

The government decreed that
on the anniversary of his birth
the people should observe
two minutes pandemonium
    Norman MacCaig (1910–1996), After His Death,
    on Hugh MacDiarmid

She was brown eggs, black skirts
and a keeper of threepenny bits
in a teapot.
    Norman MacCaig, Aunt Julia

There's a lesson here, I thought, climbing into the pulpit I
keep in my mind.
    Norman MacCaig, Country Dance

No murder'd Beast within his bowels groans
    Sir George Mackenzie (1636–1691), Caelia's Country
    House and Closet, *on a vegetarian*

My heart is a lonely hunter, that hunts on a lonely hill.
    Fiona MacLeod (William Sharp, 1855–1905), From the
Hills of Dream

an awkward, rusticated jungle wallah
    Lachlan Macquarie (1762–1784), Governor of New South
    Wales, describing how he felt on a visit to London

James Hutton, that true son of fire
    Edwin Morgan, Theory of the Earth

What Knox really did was to rob Scotland of all the
benefits of the Renaissance.
    Edwin Muir (1887–1959), John Knox

I knew he was one of the Macfarlanes. There were ten Macfarlanes, all men, except one, and he was a valet, but the family did their best to conceal the fact, and said he was away on the yachts.

    Neil Munro (1864–1930), The Vital Spark

'He iss not a brat of a boy, I admit,' said the Captain, 'but he's in the prime o' life and cheneral agility.'

    Neil Munro, In Highland Harbours with Para Handy

'I'm nae phenomena; I'm jist Nature; jist the Rale Oreeginal.'

    Neil Munro, Erchie, My Droll Friend

'Fat does he dee? Ye micht as weel speir fat I dee mysel', The things he hisna time to dee is easier to tell'

    Charles Murray (1864–1941), Docken Afore His Peers

A penniless lass wi' a lang pedigree

    Lady Nairne (1766–1845), The Laird o'Cockpen

I was a small, fat boy in a kilt with, as I saw it, limited career options … Half-human, half-traybake I may have been, but I was still keen to impress.

    Don Paterson (1963–), quoted in The Observer, *20 December 2009*

With one hand he put a penny in the urn of Poverty, and with the other he took a shilling out.

    Robert Pollok (1798–1827), The Course of Time, *on a landlord*

He scorned carriages on the ground of its being unmannerly to 'sit in a box drawn by brutes'.

    Dean E.B. Ramsay (1793–1872), Reminiscences of Scottish Life and Character, *on Lord Monboddo*

If a person is famous, it is superfluous to point out the fact. If he is not, then it is a lie. The word is not to be used on the BBC.
   Lord Reith (1889–1971), first Director-General of the BBC

And this is aa the life he kens there is.
   Tom Scott (1918–1995), Auld Sanct-Aundrians

My foot is on my native heath, and my name is MacGregor.
   Sir Walter Scott (1771–1832), Rob Roy

And there was Claverhouse, as beautiful as when he lived, with his long dark, curled locks streaming down over his laced buff-coat, and his left hand always on his right spule-blade, to hide the wound that the silver bullet had made.
   Sir Walter Scott, Redgauntlet

Up to her University days she carried the conviction that there was something about Scotland in the Bible.
   Nan Shepherd (1893–1981), Quarry Wood

He has less nonsense in his head than any man living.
   Adam Smith (1723–1790), quoted in Lord Brougham,
   Lives of Men of Letters and Science in the Reign of George III, *on Joseph Black (1728–1799)*

Upon the whole, I have always considered him, both in his lifetime and since his death, as approximating as nearly to the idea of a perfectly wise and virtuous man, as perhaps the nature of human frailty will permit.
   Adam Smith, letter to William Strachan, 1776,
   on David Hume (1711–1776)

I would rather be remembered by a song than by a victory.
   Alexander Smith (1830–1867), Dreamthorp

From my experience of life I believe my personal motto
should be 'Beware of men bearing flowers'.
  Muriel Spark (1918–2006) Curriculum Vitae

... the nicest boy who ever committed the sin of whisky.
Muriel Spark, A Sad Tale's Best for Winter

To this day his name smacks of the gallows.
  Robert Louis Stevenson (1850–1894), Some Portraits by
  Raeburn, *on Lord Braxfield*

Looking so cool,
his greed is hard to conceal,
he's fresh out of law school,
you've given him a licence to steal.
  Al Stewart (1945–), Scottish-born US lyricist and musician

An haena ye heard man, o' Barochan Jean,
How death an starvation cam' ower the haill nation:
She wrocht such mischief wi' her twa pawky e'en.
  Robert Tannahill (1774–1810), Barochan Jean

Five foot six, an unlucky thirteen stone ... a sixth rate
mathematician, a second-rate physicist, a second-rate
engineer, a bit of a meteorologist, something of a journalist,
a plausible salesman of ideas, liking to believe that there is
some poetry in my physics and some physics in my poetry.
  *Sir Robert Watson-Watt (1892–1973), in a radio broadcast,
  about himself*

We called Johnny 'Mother Superior' because ay the length
ay time he'd hud his habit.
  Irvine Welsh (1957–), Trainspotting

The Spirit of Scotland

My son, I tell thee truthfully,
No good is like to liberty.
Then never live in slavery
   Traditional, ascribed to William Wallace (c.1270–1305)

But after all, if the prince shall leave these principles he
hath so nobly pursued, and consent that we or our
kingdom be subjected to the king or people of England, we
will immediately endeavour to expel him as our enemy, and
as the subverter both of his own and our rights, and will
make another king who will defend our liberties. For as
long as there shall but one hundred of us remain alive, we
will never consent to subject ourselves to the dominion of
the English. For it is not glory, it is not riches, neither is it
honour, but it is liberty alone that we fight and contend for,
which no honest man will lose but with his life.
   The Declaration of Arbroath, *1320, from Latin*

From the lone sheiling on the misty island
Mountains divide us, and a waste of seas –
Yet still the blood is strong, the heart is Highland,
And we in dreams behold the Hebrides.
   Anonymous, Canadian Boat Song

A! fredome is a noble thing!
Fredome maiss man to haif liking:
Fredome all solace to man giffis,
He levis at ease that freely levis!
A noble heart may haif nane ease,
Nae ellis nocht that may him please,
Gif fredome failye
   John Barbour (c.1320–1395), The Brus

None can destroy Scotland, save Scotland's self.
   Lord Belhaven (1656–1708), speech in Parliament, 1706

She's a puir auld wife wi' little to give,
And rather stint o' caressin';
But she's shown us how honest lives we may live,
And sent us out wi' her blessin'.
William Black (1841–1898), Shouther to Shouther

... land of the omnipotent No
Alan Bold (1943–1998), A Memory of Death

And for my dear lov'd Land o' Cakes,
I pray with holy fire:
Lord, send a rough-shod troop o' Hell
O'er a' wad Scotland buy or sell,
To grind them in the mire!
Robert Burns (1759–1796), Election Ballad

... the story of Wallace poured a Scottish prejudice in my
veins which will boil along there till the floodgates of life
shut in eternal rest.
Robert Burns, letter to Dr John Moore (August 1787)

Our fathers fought, so runs the glorious tale,
To save you, country mine, from tyrants rash,
And now their bones and you are up for sale,
The smartest bidder buys for ready cash.
J.R. Christie, My Native Land *(c.1910)*

Land of polluted river,
Bloodshot eyes and sodden liver
Land of my heart forever
Scotland the Brave.
Sir Billy Connolly (1942–), quoted in Jonathan Margolis,
The Big Yin *(1994)*

Hame, hame, hame, hame, fain wad I be!
Hame, hame, hame, hame, to my ain countrie!
Allan Cunningham (1784–1842), Hame, Hame, Hame

I go wheresoever the shade of Montrose will direct me.
John Graham, Viscount Dundee (1648–1690),
18 March 1689

In the garb of old Gaul, wi' the fire of old Rome,
From the heath-covered mountains of Scotia we come.
Henry Erskine (1720–1765), In the Garb of Old Gaul

The Scots deserve no pity, if they voluntarily surrender
their united and separate interests to the Mercy of an
united Parliament, where the English have so vast a
Majority
Andrew Fletcher of Saltoun (1656–1716), State of the
Controversy Betwixt United and Separate Parliaments
(1706)

It is only fit for the slaves who sold it.
Andrew Fletcher of Saltoun, quoted in G.W.T. Ormond,
Fletcher of Saltoun *(1897), on Scotland after the Union*

It grows near the seashore, on banks, in clefts, but above all
on the little green braes bordered with hazel-woods. It
rarely reaches more than two feet in height, is neither white
nor cream so much as old ivory; unassuming, modest, and
known as the white rose of Scotland.
Neil Gunn (1891–1973), Highland Pack

Towering in gallant fame,
Scotland, my mountain hame –
High may your proud banners gloriously wave!
Cliff Hanley (1922–1999), Scotland the Brave

From the damp shieling on the draggled island
Mountains divide you, and no end of seas.
But, though your heart is genuinely Highland,
Still, you're in luck to be away from these!
Andrew Lang (1844–1912), To Fiona

Scotland's an attitude of mind.
Maurice Lindsay (1918–2009), Speaking of Scotland

He canna Scotland see wha yet
Canna see the Infinite,
And Scotland in true scale to it.
Hugh MacDiarmid (1892–1978), A Drunk Man Looks at the Thistle

It has suffered in the past, and is suffering now, from too much England.
A.G. Macdonell (1895–1941), My Scotland

Scottishness isn't some pedigree lineage: it's a mongrel tradition.
William McIlvanney (1936–2015), at a SNP rally, 1992

Il faut cultiver notre chardon.
Agnes Mure Mackenzie (1891–1955)

... the little band striving
When giving in would be good sense.
Sorley Maclean (1911–1996), A Poem Made When the Gaelic Society of Inverness Was 100 Years Old

No other country has fallen so hard for its own image in the funfair mirror. Tartan rock, and a Scottie dog for every pot.
Candia MacWilliam (1957–), A Case of Knives

As far as I'm concerned, Scotland will be reborn when the last minister is strangled with the last copy of the Sunday Post.
Tom Nairn (1932–1963), 'The Three Dreams of Scottish Nationalism', in K. Miller, Memoirs of a Modern Scotland (1970)

Fecht for Britain? Hoot, awa!
For Bonnie Scotland? Imph, man, na!
For Lochnagar? Wi' clook and claw!
    J.C. Milne, quoted in H. Brown,
    Poems of the Scottish Hills *(1982)*

This is a difficult country, and our home.
    Edwin Muir (1887–1959), The Difficult Land

Of Scotland's king I haud my hoose,
He pays me meat and fee;
And I will keep my gude auld hoose,
While my hoose will keep me.
    'Black' Agnes Randolph, Countess of March
    (fl. 14th century), to the besiegers of Dunbar Castle

The solitudes of land and sea assuage
My quenchless thirst for freedom unconfined;
With independent heart and mind
Hold I my heritage.
    Robert Rendall (1898–1967), Orkney Crofter

There is a storm coming that shall try your foundations.
Scotland must be rid of Scotland before the delivery come.
    James Renwick (1662–1688), Cameronian leader,
    at his execution

If we don't have some self-respect we
Might as well be in the ground
If we've got nothin' else at least
We've got our pride.
    Tony Roper (1941–), 'Pride', from The Steamie *(1987)*

Breathes there the man with soul so dead
Who never to himself hath said,
This is my own, my native land!
    Sir Walter Scott, The Lay of the Last Minstrel

O Caledonia! stern and wild,
Meet nurse for a poetic child!
Land of brown heath and shaggy wood;
Land of the mountain and the flood!
   Sir Walter Scott, The Lay of the Last Minstrel

There are too many 90-minute patriots whose nationalist
outpourings are expressed only at major sporting events.
   Jim Sillars (1937–)

This is the land God gave to Andy Stewart –
   Iain Crichton Smith (1928–1998),
   The White Air of March

... my young nephew Patrick, the taciturn Scot of all the
Scots; he who, at the age of three, held up before a mirror
by his grandmother and asked by her, 'Wha's that?' had
lived up to the highest tradition of the Scots by his riposte,
'Wha wad it be?'
   Sir Robert Watson-Watt (1892–1973),
   Three Steps to Victory

O Flower of Scotland
When will we see your like again
That fought and died for
Your wee bit hill and glen ...
These days are past now
And in the past they must remain,
But we can still rise now,
And be a nation again.
   Roy Williamson (1936–1990), Flower of Scotland (1969)

Sport and Pastimes

Everywhere we go-o!
People want to know-ow
Who the hell we a-are
And where we come from.
We're the Tartan Army,
We're mental and we're barmy.
>   *Anonymous, 'Everywhere We Go', Quoted in Ian Black,*
>   Tales of the Tartan Army (*1997*)

The grouse shooters were often rather pathetic people,
going through a ritual imposed on them because they could
afford it ... They were stung, by everything and everybody.
>   *John R. Allan (1906–1986)*, Farmer's Boy

Th' athletic fool to whom what Heav'n denied
Of soul is well compensated in limbs ...
The men of better clay and finer mould
Know nature, feel the human dignity,
And scorn to vie with oxen or with apes.
>   *John Armstrong (c.1709–1779)*,
>   The Art of Preserving Health

The charm of fishing is that it is the pursuit of what is
elusive but attainable: a perpetual series of occasions for
hope.
>   *John Buchan (1875–1940)*

My son was born to play for Scotland. He has all the
qualities, a massive ego, a criminal record, an appalling
drink problem, and he's not very good at football.
>   *'Mrs Alice Cosgrove', quoted on the back cover of Stuart*
>   *Cosgrove*, Hampden Babylon (*1991*)

Football management these days is like a nuclear war. No winners, only survivors.
Tommy Docherty (1928–2020), quoted in Peter Ball and Phil Shaw, The Umbro Book of Football Quotations *(1993)*

The only game in which you can put on weight while playing it.
Tommy Docherty, on cricket

If Johnson had deliberately intended an attack on the referee, his right foot would not have missed the target.
F.A. Disciplinary Report on Willie 'Wee Bud' Johnson (1976), quoted in S. Cosgrove, Hampden Babylon *(1991)*

The doctor said, 'This child's very ill. Have to get him to hospital.' 'I canny take him,' the man says. 'Celtic are playing Leeds United tonight.'
Hugh Ferrie, Celtic supporter, quoted in S. Walsh, Voices of the Old Firm *(1995)*

Play Up, Play Up, And Get Tore In
George Macdonald Fraser (1925–2008), title of short story

Would you also be good enough to bring your ball with you in case of any breake down, and thus prevent interruptsion. Hoping the weather will favour the Thistle and Queen.
Robert Gardner, Letter to the Secretary of Thistle FC, Glasgow, June 1867, arranging the first known inter-club football game in Scotland

Bi' ma knees is skint and bluddan,
an ma breeks they want the seat,
jings! ye get mair nir ye're eftir,
pleyan fi'baw in the street.
Robert Garioch (Robert Garioch Sutherland, 1909–1981), Fi'baw in the Street

Even in the Foreign Office I could set my watch by the evening flight of the ducks from St James's Park – over the Horse Guards Parade to the Thames estuary – and select a right and a left with my imaginary gun.
Lord Home (1903–1995), Border Reflections

Why is it that I play at all?
Let memory remind me
How once I smote upon my ball,
And bunkered it – *behind me*.
Andrew Lang (1844–1912), Off My Game

The secret of my success over the four hundred metres is that I run the first two hundred metres as hard as I can. Then, for the second two hundred metres, with God's help, I run faster.
Eric H. Liddell (1902–1945), on winning the Olympic gold medal (1924)

All I've got against it is that it takes you so far from the clubhouse.
Eric Linklater (1899–1974), on golf

Five grand a week? That's my kind of pressure.
Lou Macari (1949–), quoted in K. Macdonald,
Scottish Football Quotations, *1994*

The game's a bogey!
Children's cry, also used as a play title by John McGrath, 1974

Oh, he's fitba' crazy, he's fitba' mad
And the fitba' it has robbed him of the wee bit sense he had.
And it would take a dozen skivvies, his clothes tae wash and scrub,
Since oor Jock became a member of that terrible football club.
James Curran (19thc), revised by Jimmie MacGregor (1930–), Fitba' Crazy

Right, let's hospitalise these bastards!

Alastair McHarg, rugby international, in a match against England, 1971, quoted by Quintin Dunlop, Scotsman, *5 March 2011*

... the game is hopelessly ill-equipped to carry the burden of emotional expression the Scots seek to load upon it. What is hurting so many now is the realisation that something they believed to be a metaphor for their pride has all along been a metaphor for their desperation.

Hugh McIlvanney (1934–2019), McIlvanney on Football

Eck: ... This is where I come to do what the Scots are best at.
Willie: Shinty?
Eck: Moping.

John McKay (1965–), Dead Dad Dog

If I ask the players for less than perfection they'll definitely give me less.

Jim McLean, football manager, quoted in K. Macdonald, Scottish Football Quotations *(1994)*

Among the Scots, licking of wounds is second only to football as a national sport, ecstasy occurring when the two activities merge (as they often do) into one.

Tom Nairn (1932–1963), The Guardian, *May 1986*

Golf is not a relaxation, golf is everything, golf is a philosophy, it's a religion, absolutely, I mean really absolutely.

Sir Bob Reid (1934–), quoted in the Sunday Times *(November 1989)*

Some people think football is a matter of life and death ... I can assure them it is much more serious than that.

Bill Shankly (1914–1981), quoted in The Guardian, *1973*

I don't drop players. I make changes.
Bill Shankly, quoted in The Guardian, *1973*

If you're in the penalty area and don't know what to do
with the ball, put it in the net and we'll discuss the options
later.
Bill Shankly, quoted by Alastair Mackay in
The Scotsman *(July 1998)*

The trouble with you, son, is that your brains are all in
your head.
Bill Shankly to a Liverpool player, 1967

I've been basically honest in a game in which it's sometimes
difficult to be honest. Sometimes you've got to tell a little
white lie to get over a little troublesome period of time.
Bill Shankly

The ultimate Scottish international team would be: Knox,
Wallace, Bruce, Burns, Montrose, Dunbar, Adam, Napier,
Smith, Telford and Stewart. Absolute certainty of salvation
in goal; tigerish tackling and devilish cunning at full back; a
centre back of legendary courage ... the left winger can be
Charles Edward, Lachie, or Jackie, they could all shift a bit
when the going was good or bad.
W. Gordon Smith (1928–1996), This is My Country *(1976)*

I get frustrated with certain aspects of the game. But there's
things that dekight me. It's just the uncertainty of it all.
Graeme Souness (1953–),

We all end up yesterday's men in this business.
Jock Stein (1922–1985), quoted in Archie Macpherson,
The Great Derbies

Glaswegian definition of an atheist – a man who goes to a
Celtic–Rangers match to watch the football.
Sandy Strang (1951–2017), quoted in S. Walsh,
Voices of Old Firm *(1995)*

Thoughts, Wishes and Reflections

What is hotter than fire? The face of an hospitable man,
when strangers come, and there is nought to offer.
Anonymous, from 'Fionn's Questions', quoted by
Amy Murray in Father Allan's Island *(1936)*

Steal ane cow, twa cow, tat be common tief. Steal hundred
cow, tat be shentleman drover.
Anonymous Highlander, 18th century

O that the peats would cut themselves,
The fish jump on the shore.
And that I in my bed could lie
And sleep for ever more.
Anonymous, The Crofter's Prayer

Even to be happy is a dangerous thing.
Sir William Alexander (c.1567–1640), Darius

Its all one thing, both tends unto one Scope
To live upon Tabacco and on hope,
The one's but smoake, the other is but wind.
Sir Robert Ayton (1570–1638), Upone Tabacco

Endurance is not just the ability to bear a hard thing, but to
turn it into glory.
William Barclay (1907–1978), in The British Weekly

As soon as you can say what you think, and not what some
other person has thought for you, you are on the way to
being a remarkable man.
Sir J.M. Barrie (1860–1973), Tommy and Grizel

Two negatives make a positive but only in Scotland do two
positives make a negative: aye, right.
Frankie Boyle (1972–)

The Big House of the bairn, so enormous, majestic, what is it? just decently earning its keep as a farm. Oh, never revisit!

Ivor Brown (1891–1974), Never Go Back

O wad some Power the giftie gie us
To see oursels as ithers see us!
It wad frae monie a blunder free us,
And foolish notion.

Robert Burns (1759–1796), To a Louse

Everything's intentional. It's just filling in the dots.

David Byrne (1952–), Scottish-born US musician

'Tis distance lends enchantment to the view

Thomas Campbell (1777–1844), The Pleasures of Hope

Like pensive beauty, smiling in her tears

Thomas Campbell, The Pleasures of Hope

Like angel visits, few and far between.

Thomas Campbell, The Pleasures of Hope

Me, made after the image o' God?
Jings, but it's laughable, tae.

Joe Corrie (1894–1968), Miners' Wives

And all the gay deceased of old,
The wise, the generous, the good. . .
To match their deeds I would not strive,
But put your money, boys, on me,
For they are dead and I'm alive.

T.L. Douglas, 'A Living Dog', from
Glasgow University Poems, *1910*

What sweet delight a quiet life affords
And what it is from bondage to be free,
Far from the madding worldlings' hoarse discords

William Drummond (1585–1649), The Cypresse Grove

The stars are filming us for no-one.
  Carol Ann Duffy (1955–)

Excess of thocht does me mischeif.
  William Dunbar (c.1460–c.1520), To the King

The sea, I think, is lazy,
It just obeys the moon
  Ian Hamilton Finlay (1925–1996), Mansie Considers the
  Sea, in the Manner of Hugh MacDiarmid

To every man the hardest form of slavery is to serve as a
slave in one's own native country, there where one was
wont to be free lord.
  John Fordun (d.1385), Scotichronicon,
  translated from Latin

... good triumphs and the villain bites the dust. If anyone
believes that, the story of the Border Reivers should
convince him otherwise. Its moral is clear: there is little
justice to be had. The good man survives, if he is lucky, but
the villain becomes the first Lord Roxburgh.
  George Macdonald Fraser (1925–2008),
  The Steel Bonnets (*1971*)

The posters show my country blonde and green,
Like some sweet siren, but the travellers know
How dull the shale sky is, the airs how keen
  G.S. Fraser (1915–1980), Meditation of a Patriot

Now up in the mornin's no for me,
Up in the mornin' early;
When snaw blaws into the chimley cheek,
Wha'd rise in the mornin' early?
  John Hamilton (1761–1814), Up in the Morning Early

Tiresome 'tis to be a dreamer.
When will it be time to dine?
James Hedderwick (1814–1897), The Villa by the Sea

I carena muckle for folk that bairns and dogs dinna like.
James Hogg (1770–1835), quoted in Margaret Garden,
Memorials of James Hogg

An' what'll I get when my mither kens
Violet Jacob (1863–1946), The End O't

'It cam wi a lass, and it'll gang wi a lass'
*King James V (1512–1542), on his deathbed, learning that
his new-born heir was a girl*

The party's almost over. Though at times a trifle odd, I've
thoroughly enjoyed it. Thank you for having me, God.
Maurice Lindsay (1918–2009), To Catch the Last Post

What more lovely than to be alone
With a Teasmade, a radio and a telephone?
Liz Lochhead (1947–), Heartbreak Hotel

Nae man or movement's worth a damn unless
The movement 'ud gang on withoot him if
He de'ed the morn.
Hugh MacDiarmid (C.M. Grieve, 1892–1978),
Depth and the Chthonian Image

They sang that never was sadness
But it melted and passed away;
They sang that never was darkness
But in came the conquering day.
George Macdonald (1824–1905), The Old Garden

I mauna cuddle in the wyme o' yesterdays.
Alastair Mackie (1925–1995), Aiberdeen Street

Therefore put quite away
All heaviness of thocht:
Thoch we murne nicht and day
It will avail us nocht.
Sir Richard Maitland (1496–1586),
Advice to Leesome Merriness

… no-one need expect to be original simply by being
absurd. There is a cycle in nonsense … which ever and
anon brings back the delusions and error of an earlier time.
Hugh Miller (1820–1856), The Testimony of the Rocks

We bear the lot of nations,
Of times and races,
Because we watched the wrong
Last too long
With non-commital faces.
Edwin Muir (1887–1959), The Refugees

God has to nearly kill us sometimes, to teach us lessons.
John Muir (1838–1914), quoted in National Parks
Magazine (*US*), *2007*

On one occasion he declared that he was richer than
magnate E. H. Harriman: 'I have all the money I want and
he hasn't.'
John Muir, quoted in C. Fadiman, The Little Brown
Book of Anecdotes (*1985*)

Temptations come, as a general rule, when they are sought.
Margaret Oliphant (1828–1897), Miss Marjoribanks

There can be no peace in the world so long as a large
proportion of the population lack the necessities of life and
believe that a change of the political and economic system
will make them available. World peace must be based on
world plenty.
John Boyd Orr (1880–1971)

The future is not what it used to be.
    Sir Malcolm Rifkind (1946–), Tory politician

Sometimes, if you want things to stay the same, things have to change.
    Sir Malcolm Rifkind, BBC News Channel, May 2005

Whit trasherie will I turn up the day?
    Christopher Rush (1944–), Monday Morning

But THOU hast said, The blood of goat,
The flash of rams I will not prize;
A contrite heart, a humble thought,
Are mine accepted sacrifice.
    Sir Walter Scott (1771–1832), 'Rebecca's Hymn', *from*
    Ivanhoe

Sorrow remembers us when day is done
    Iain Crichton Smith (1928–1998), When Day is Done

We ever new, we ever young,
We happy creatures of a day!
    C.H. Sorley (1895–1915), Untitled Poem

Darkness is your only door;
Gang doun wi' a sang, gang doun.
    William Soutar (1898–1943), Song

Ah! forgive me, fellow-creatures,
If I mock when you are gone;
And if sometimes at life's concert
I would rather sit alone
    William Soutar, Impromptu in an Eremitic Mood

But oh! what a cruel thing is a farce to those engaged in it!
    Robert Louis Stevenson (1850–1894),
    Travels With a Donkey

The faculty of imagination is the great spring of human activity ... Destroy this faculty, and the condition of man will become as stationary as that of the brutes.

Dugald Stewart (1753–1828), Elements of the Philosophy of the Human Mind

The world rolls round for ever like a mill;
It grinds out death and life and good and ill;
It has no purpose, heart or mind or will.

James Thomson (1834–1882), The City of Dreadful Night

Noo slings aboot an' stars a' oot, an' auld moon chowin' sin,
Here ye wonner really at the din,
As fit aboot of ebbs salute, and fetters all the score,
Hyfon pland often really soar.

Thomas Thomson (1837–1924), Hyfons, Hyfons

Aye, it's on the highways
The feck o' life maun gang:
But aye it's frae the byways
Comes hame the happy sang.

Walter Wingate (1865–1918), Highways and Byways

Toasts and Greetings

May the best ye've ever seen
Be the worst ye ever see.

Traditional

May the mouse never leave our meal pock wi' the tear in its eye.

Traditional

Would it not be the beautiful thing now
If you were coming instead of going?

Traditional island farewell, from Gaelic

Here's to the king, sir,
Ye ken wha I mean, sir.
Jacobite toast

The King ower the Water.
Jacobite toast, passing a glass over a water-jug

The little gentleman in black velvet.
*Jacobite toast, to the mole on whose hill King William III's
horse stumbled, causing his death*

For auld lang syne, my dear,
For auld lang syne,
We'll tak' a cup o' kindness yet,
For auld lang syne.
Robert Burns (1759–1796), Auld Lang Syne

Fair fa' your honest, sonsie face,
Great chieftain o' the pudding-race!
Robert Burns, Address to a Haggis

Napoleon is a tyrant, a monster, the sworn foe of our
nation. But gentlemen – he once shot a publisher.
*Thomas Campbell (1777–1844), proposing a toast to
Bonaparte at a writers' dinner*

Good night, and joy be wi' you a';
We'll maybe meet again the morn.
James Hogg (1770–1835), Good Night, and Joy Be Wi' You

The traditional Orkney invitation to a visitor was, 'Put in
thee hand.'
Edwin Muir (1887–1959), Autobiography

Plenty herring, plenty meal,
Plenty peat to fill her creel –
Plenty bonny bairns as weel,
That's the toast for Mairi.
Sir Hugh S. Roberton (1874–1952), The Lewis Bridal Song

Transport and Travel

Had you seen these roads before they were made,
You would lift up your hands and bless General Wade.
Anonymous, lines on the military roads constructed under
General George Wade during 1726–37

The earth belongs unto the Lord,
And all that it contains;
Except the Western Isles alone,
And they are all MacBrayne's.
Anonymous rhyme on the MacBrayne Steamship
Company, 20th century

I am travelling with a general desire to improve myself.
James Boswell (1740–1795), Letter to Jean-Jacques
Rousseau, December 1764

In the event of a cabin failure, oxygen masks will drop from
the ceiling, and untangling them will annoy you before you
die.
Frankie Boyle (1972–)

A grand old boat is the Waverley,
She'll tak ye doon tae Rothesay and be back for tea,
The way she did when ye were wee.
Jim Brown, 'The Waverley Polka', in Ewan MacVicar,
One Singer, One Song *(1990)*

If any man wants to be happy, I advise him to get a public
allowance for travelling.
Henry Thomas Cockburn (1779–1854), Circuit Journeys

Oh, ye should hear his manly voice when cryin' ilka day,
'The ither side for Wilsontown, Carnwath, and Auchengray!'
An' then he's aye sae cheery, aye the foremost i' the ploy:
My bonnie porter laddie wi' the green corduroy.
T.S. Denholm, 'The Green Corduroy', in Caledonian
Railway *Christmas Annual, 1909*

I remember a crofter on the island of Eigg, who, when asked when the steamer would arrive, replied at once, 'Weel, she'll be comin' sometimes sooner, and whiles earlier, and sometimes before that again.'

Sir Archibald Geikie (1835–1924), Scottish Reminiscences

But I need the rides most, hurling warm through all weathers and seasons, with a paperback thriller on my lap, and always Scotland outside the window in more changes of scenery in ten miles than England in fifteen or Europe in twenty, or India, America or Russia in a hundred.

Alasdair Gray (1934–2019), 1982 Janine

No doubt he'd come home by instinct, the poor man's taxi.

Brian McCabe (1951–), The Other McCoy

I don't like this, being carried sideways through the night. I feel wrong and helpless – like a timber broadside in a fast stream.

Norman MacCaig (1910–1996), Sleeping Compartment

I'll tak ye on the road again,
When yellow's on the broom.

Adam McNaughtan, When Yellow's On the Broom (2001)

… we were graciously received by Lady Seafield, to whom we explained the purport of our visit. She very decidedly told us she 'hated railways,' – they brought together such an objectionable variety of people. Posting, in her opinion, with four horses, was the perfection of travelling.

Joseph Mitchell (1803–1883), Reminiscences of
  My Life in the Highlands

May God bless the bark of Clan-Ranald
The first day she floats on the brine:
Himself and his strong men to man her –
The heroes whom none can outshine.

Alexander Nicolson (1827–1893), The Galley of
  Clanranald, *from the Gaelic of Alastair Macdonald*

The end of the world is near when the MacBrayne's ship
will be on time.
  Iain Crichton Smith (1928–1998), Thoughts of Murdo

the silent ferryman standing in the stern
clutching his coat about him like old iron.
  Iain Crichton Smith, By Ferry to the Island

I travel not to go anywhere, but to go. I travel for travel's
sake. The great affair is to move.
  Robert Louis Stevenson (1850–1894) Travels with a Donkey

To travel hopefully is a better thing than to arrive.
  Robert Louis Stevenson, Virginibus Puerisque

As we rush, as we rush in the train,
The trees and the houses go wheeling back,
But the starry heavens above the plain
Come flying in on our track.
  James Thomson (1834–1882), The Train

Highways for eident feet,
That hae their mile to gae.
  Walter Wingate (1865–1918), Highways and Byways

War and Warriors

In doubtsome victory they dealt;
The bludy battle lasted long;
Ilk man his neighbour's force there felt
The weakest oft-times got the wrong.
  Anonymous, The Battle of Harlaw

'Fight on, my men,' says Sir Andrew Barton,
'I am hurt, but I am not slain;
I'le lay me down and bleed awhile,
And then I'le rise and fight again.'
  Anonymous, Sir Andrew Barton

Fair maiden Lylliard lies under this stane
Little was her stature but great was her fame
Upon the English louns she laid many thumps,
And when her legs were cuttit off she fought upon the stumps.
Inscription recorded from 'Lilliard's Stone', Midlothian

Teribus ye teri odin,
Sons of heroes slain at Flodden,
Imitating Border bowmen,
Aye defend your rights and common.
Traditional Hawick rhyme, quoted in Charles Mackay,
Poetry and Humour of the Scottish Language (*1882*)

I faught at land, I faught at sea,
At hame I faught my aunty, O;
But I met the devil and Dundee,
On the braes o' Killiecrankie, O
Anonymous, on the battle of Killiecrankie (26 July 1689)

Everybody else took the road he liked best
Contemporary comment on the end of the 1715 Rising,
following the secret departure of the 'Old Pretender' and the
Earl of Mar, quoted in C. Stewart Black, Scottish Battles
(*1936*)

A Gordon for me, a Gordon for me:
If you're no' a Gordon you're nae use to me.
The Black Watch are braw, the Seaforths and a',
But the cocky wee Gordon's the pride o' them a'.
Anonymous, A Gordon for Me

The wind may blaw, the cock may craw,
The rain may rain, and the snaw may snaw;
But ye winna frichten Jock McGraw,
The stoutest man in the Forty-Twa.
Anonymous, The Stoutest Man in the Forty-Twa

'They're a' out o' step but oor Jock!'
> *Apocryphal mother watching soldiers at drill through the railings of a Glasgow barracks*

For the king had said him rudely
That ane rose of his chaplet
Was fallen
> *John Barbour (c.1320–1395), The Brus: Bruce's rebuke to the Earl of Moray on the field of Bannockburn, 1314*

There is no such thing as an inevitable war. If war comes it will be from failure of human wisdom.
> *Andrew Bonar Law (1858–1923), speech*

Scots, wha hae wi' Wallace bled,
Scots, wham Bruce has aften led,
Welcome to your gory bed,
Or to victory.
> *Robert Burns (1759–1796), Bruce's Address to His Army Before Bannockburn*

I once was a maid, tho' I cannot tell when,
And still my delight is in proper young men;
Some one of a troop of dragoons was my daddie,
No wonder I'm fond of a sodger laddie.
> *Robert Burns, The Jolly Beggars*

Cock up your beaver, and cock it fu' sprush,
We'll over the Border and gie them a brush
> *Robert Burns, Cock Up Your Beaver*

Ye hypocrites! are these your pranks?
To murder men, and gie God thanks!
For shame! Gie o'er – proceed no farther –
God won't accept your thanks for murther.
> *Robert Burns, Verses Written on a Pane of Glass on the the Occasion of a National Thanksgiving for a Naval Victory*

'Ninety-third! Ninety-third! Damn all that eagerness.'
> *Sir Colin Campbell (1792–1863), to the Argylls at Balaclava*
> (October 1854), *quoted in C. Woodham-Smith*, The
> Reason Why (*1953*)

'Men, remember there is no retreat from here. You must die where you stand.'
> *Sir Colin Campbell, to the Argylls at Balaclava (October*
> *1854), quoted in C. Woodham-Smith*, The Reason Why
> (*1953*)

When was a war not a war? When it was carried on by means of barbarism.
> *Sir Henry Campbell-Bannerman (1836–1908), Speech to the*
> *National Reform Union Dinner, June 1901, on the Boer War*

Victory belongs to those who hold out the longest.
> *Field Marshal Earl Haig (1861–1928), Order to the British*
> *Expeditionary Force, April 1918*

Never volunteer for nothing
> *Hamish Henderson (1919–2002),* Fort Capuzzo

The main force used in the evolving world of humanity has hitherto been applied in the form of war.
> *Sir Arthur Keith (1866–1955)* Evolution and Ethics

Every bullet has its billet;
Many bullets more than one.
God! Perhaps I killed a mother,
When I killed a mother's son.
> *Joseph Lee (1876–1949),* The Bullet

They are a song in the blood of all true men.
> *Hugh MacDiarmid (C.M. Grieve, 1892–1978),*
> The International Brigades

'I will follow you to death, were there no other to draw a
sword in your cause.'
  Ronald MacDonald (fl. mid 18th century), quoted in
  Dugald Mitchell, History of the Highlands and Gaelic
  Scotland *(1900), to Prince Charles Edward Stuart, July*
  1745

Fat civilians wishing they
'Could go and fight the Hun.'
Can't you see them thanking God
That they're over forty-one?
  E.A. Mackintosh (1893–1916), Recruiting

Lads, you're wanted. Come and die.
E.A. Mackintosh, Recruiting

Lest we see a worse thing than it is to die,
Live ourselves and see our friends cold beneath the sky,
God grant that we too be lying there in wind and mud and
    rain
Before the broken regiments come stumbling back again.
  E.A. Mackintosh, Before the Summer

The only war that is worth waging is the Class War
  John Maclean (1879–1923), The Vanguard

There's some say that we wan,
Some say that they wan,
Some say that nane wan at a', man;
But o' ae thing I'm sure,
That at Sheriffmuir,
A battle there was that I saw, man.
And we ran, and they ran,
And they ran, and we ran,
And they ran and we ran awa', man.
  Murdoch MacLennan (fl. early 18th century),
  Sheriffmuir *(1715)*

Tonight's the night – if the lads are the lads!
The Macnab's rallying cry to his twelve sons, quoted in
Augustus Muir, Heather Track and High Road (*1944*)

There's nothing noo in the heids o' the gyurls but sodgers.
But ye canna blame the craturs! There's something smert
aboot the kilt and the cockit bonnet.
Neil Munro (1864–1930),
Hurricane Jack of the Vital Spark

Gin danger's there, we'll thole our share,
Gi'es but the weapons, we've the will
Ayont the main to prove again,
Auld Scotland counts for something still.
Charles Murray (1864–1941), A Sough of War

There are more than birds on the hill tonight,
And more than winds on the plain!
The threat of the Scotts has filled the moss,
'There will be moonlight again.'
Will H. Ogilvie (1869–1963), The Blades of Harden

Hail to the Chief who in triumph advances!
Sir Walter Scott (1771–1832), The Lady of the Lake

… the stern joy which warriors feel
In foemen worthy of their steel.
Sir Walter Scott, The Lady of the Lake

I hae swaggered wi' a' thae arms, and muskets, and pistols,
buff-coats and bandoliers, lang eneugh, and I like the
pleugh-paidle a hantle better.
Sir Walter Scott, Old Mortality

'Aye, if ye had fower legs ye wouldnae stand there lang.'
Wat Scott of Harden (fl. late 16th century), quoted in
G.M. Fraser, The Steel Bonnets (*1971*), *remark made on*
passing a haystack on the way home from an English raid

The security of every society must always depend, more or less, upon the martial spirit of the great body of the people.
Adam Smith (1723–1790), The Wealth of Nations

Doutless he deed for Scotland's life;
Doutless the statesmen dinna lee;
But och tis sair begrutten pride,
And wersh the wine o' victorie!
Sydney Goodsir Smith (1915–1975), The Mither's Lament

The captain's all right, really. A touch of the toasted tea-breid. You know the type.
W. Gordon Smith (1928–1996), Mr Jock (1987)

As a nation we've fallen in and marched behind some damned funny folk.
W. Gordon Smith, Mr Jock

Earth that blossom'd and was glad
'Neath the cross that Christ had,
Shall rejoice and blossom too
When the bullet reaches you.
C.H. Sorley (1895–1915), Untitled Poem

Machines of death from east to west
Drone through the darkened sky;
Machines of death from west to east
Through the same darkness fly ...
They leave a ruin; and they meet
A ruin on return
William Soutar (1898–1943), Revelation

'... it may come to a fecht for it yet, Davie; and then, I'll confess I would be blythe to have you at my oxter, and I think you would be none the worse of having me at yours.'
Robert Louis Stevenson (1850–1894), Catriona

Words, Language and Speech

Baith in one.
> *Traditional. An esoteric phrase used as the 'Horseman's word', given to young farmhands on their initiation.*

Words of affection, howsoe'er express'd,
The latest spoken still are deemed the best.
> *Joanna Baillie (1762–1851)*, Address to Miss Agnes Baillie on Her Birthday

Let us treat children and fairies in a more summary manner ... Nowadays if in reading a book I come across a word beginning with 'c' or 'f' I toss it aside.
> *Sir J.M. Barrie (1860–1937)*, Speech to the Royal Literary Fund, 1930

A word, he says, is short and quick, but works
A long result
> *John Stuart Blackie (1809–1895)*, The Wise Men of Greece

Our school was in Scotland, in almost every respect a Scottish public school, and yet a strong Scottish accent was a real stigma ... When people spoke with a strong Scottish accent we would make harsh retching sounds in the base of our throats or emit loose-jawed idiot burblings.
> *William Boyd (1952–)*, Old School Ties, *on Gordonstoun School in the 1960s*

The tinkers have curious voices – angular outcast flashing accents like the cries of seagulls.
> *George Mackay Brown (1921–1996)*, Five Green Waves

It is a word, blossoming as legend, poem, story, secret, that holds a community together and gives a meaning to its life ... Decay of language is always the symptom of a more serious sickness.
> *George Mackay Brown*, An Orkney Tapestry

Most words descend in value.
Ivor Brown (1891–1974), A Word in Your Ear

Glamour … this beautiful word has been bludgeoned to death by modern showmanship … an English importation from Scotland where it had long signified magic with magical effect.
Ivor Brown, A Word in Your Ear

I can perceive without regret the gradual extinction of the ancient Scottish language, and cheerfully allow its harsh sounds to die away, and give place to the softer and more harmonious tones of the Latin.
George Buchanan (c.1506–1582), quoted in
A. L. Williamson, Scottish National Consciousness in the Age of James VI (*1979*)

The mair they talk I'm kend the better;
E'en let them clash!
Robert Burns (1759–1796),
The Poet's Welcome to His Bastart Wean

I realised that Gaelic was a missing part of my world, since with the modern Gael I share a history but not a language … his history remains mine; written into my conscience in invisible ink, in a language I have forgotten how to understand.
James Campbell, Invisible Country (*1984*)

The coldest word was once a glowing new metaphor
Thomas Carlyle (1795–1881), Past and Present

Great the blindness and the sinful darkness and ignorance and evil will of those who teach, write and foster the Gaelic speech; for to win for themselves the empty rewards of the world, they both choose and use more and more to make vain and misleading tales, lying and worldly, of the Tuath de Danann, of fighting men and champions, of Fionn MacCumhal and his heroes, and many more whom now I will not number.

John Carswell, Kirk Superintendent of Argyll (fl mid 16th century), translated from Gaelic, in the Introduction to a Gaelic translation of the Liturgy of the English Congregation at Geneva, quoted in Agnes Mure Mackenzie, Scottish Pageant 1513–1625 *(1948)*

In Scotland we live between and across languages.
Robert Crawford (1959–), Identifying Poets

… the Society's design was … not to continue the Irish language, but to wear it out, and learn the people the English tongue

Committee of the Society for the Propagation of Christian Knowledge (1720), quoted in Agnes Mure Mackenzie, Scottish Pageant 1707–1802 *(1950)*

Edinburgh, one of the few European capitals with no anti-semitism in its history, accepted them with characteristic cool interest. In its semi-slums they learned such English as they knew, which meant in fact that they grafted the debased Scots of the Edinburgh streets onto their native Yiddish to produce one of the most remarkable dialects ever spoken by man.

David Daiches (1912–2005), Two Worlds

Doric has a secret world of its own, an atmosphere I am unable to define.

A.M. Davidson (1897–1979), The Tinker's Whussel

Traist weill, to follow ane fixt sentence or matter
Is mair practic, difficil, and mair straiter,
Though thine ingyne be elevate and hie,
Than for to write all ways at libertie.
  Gavin Douglas (1475–1522), Prologue to the Aeneid,
  on translation

Telling the secret, telling, clucking and tutting,
Sighing, or saying it served her right,
the bitch! – the words and weather both are cutting
In Causewayend, on this November night.
  G.S. Fraser (1915–1980), Lean Street

A fouth o' flours may yet be fund
Wi' pains, on Caledonian grund.
Dig for their roots, or they be dead,
Fra Gretna Green to Peterhead;
And plant them quick, as soon as got,
In ae lexicographic pot;
I trou they'll soon baith live and thrive
And gie you flours eneuch belyve.
  Alexander Geddes (1737–1802), Transactions of the
  Society of Antiquaries (*1792*)

Chris would say they needn't fash, if she said it in Scots the
woman would think, Isn't that a common-like bitch at the
Manse? If she said it in English the speak would spread
round the minister's wife was putting on airs.
  Lewis Grassic Gibbon (James Leslie Mitchell, 1901–1935),
  Cloud Howe

What is the language
Using us for?
For the prevailing weather or words
Each object hides in a metaphor.
  W.S. Graham (1918–1986),
  What Is the Language Using Us For?

You can hear from my voice I don't sound particularly Scottish, so despite the fact that, as far as I know, that's what I am, I'm quite used to being asked how long I'm here for.

David Greig (1969–), BBC 'Belief' interview

Words are well adapted for description and arousing of emotions, but for many kinds of precise thought, other symbols are much better.

J.B.S. Haldane (1892–1964)

The gude auld honest mither tongue!
They kent nae ither, auld or young;
The cottar spak' it in his yaird,
An' on his rigs the gawcie laird.

Hugh Haliburton (J. Logie Robertson, 1864–1922), On the Decadence of the Scots Language, Manners and Customs

the tung has the poo'er ... whit other tung could pit glory and grimness gleich afore us?

Christopher Harvie (1944–), speech on the 75th anniversary of the Saltire Society, 16 June 2011

Would you repeat that again, sir, for it sounds sae sonorous that the words droon the ideas?

James Hogg (1770–1835), quoted in Christopher North (John Wilson, 1785–1854), 'Noctes Ambrosianae'

Since word is thrall, and thought is free,
Keep well thy tongue, I counsel thee.

King James VI (1566–1625), Ballad of Good Counsel

It is harder to take words back than it is to get a refund.

Jackie Kay (1961–), Why Don't You Stop Talking?

what's your favourite word dearie
is it wee
I hope it's wee
wee's such a nice wee word
    Tom Leonard (1944–), The Voyeur

'Learn English!' he exclaimed, 'no, never; it was my trying
to learn that language that spoilt my Scots; and as to being
silent, I will promise to hold my tongue if you will make
fools hold theirs.'
    Dr John Leyden (1775–1811), quoted in John Reith, The
    Life of Dr John Leyden *(1909), when asked, on his arrival
    in Bombay, not to discuss literature and to speak 'English'*

Douglas Young, anxious to demonstrate the living quality
of Scots, held up his empty beer glass and called to the
barman, 'Some mair.' To everyone's astonishment, the
barman presently came across carrying a long pole and
pulled open an upper window.
    Maurice Lindsay (1918–2009), Thank You for Having Me

It's soon', no' sense, that faddoms the herts o' men,
And by my sangs the rouch auld Scots I ken
E'en herts that hae nae Scots'll dirl richt thro'
As nocht else could – for here's a language rings
Wi' datchie sesames, and names for nameless things.
    Hugh MacDiarmid (C.M. Grieve, 1892–1978),
    Gairmscoile

'Tis the speech used in the Garden–
Adam left it to mankind.
    Duncan Bàn MacIntyre (1724–1812), Rann Do
    'N Ghaidhlig 'S Do 'N Phiob-Mhoir *(Ode to Gaelic and
    the Great Pipe)*

The Scotch is as spangled with vowels as a meadow with
daisies in the month of May.
    Charles Mackay (1814–1889), The Poetry and Humour
    of the Scottish Language

To me it appears undeniable that the Scotish Idiom of the British Tongue is more fit for Pleading than either the English Idiom or the French Tongue; for certainly a Pleader must use a brisk, smart and quick way of speaking ... Our Pronunciation is like ourselves, fiery, abrupt, sprightly and bold.

Sir George Mackenzie (1636–1691), What Eloquence is Fit for the Bar

It is natural for a poet to love his own language if it is the language of his ancestors and dying, even if it were a poor defective thing. Gaelic is not a poor language, in art at any rate.

Sorley Maclean (1911–1996)

You could drive a train across the Firth of Forth on her vowels.

Bruce Marshall (1899–1987), Teacup Terrace

The accent of the lowest state of Glaswegians is the ugliest one can encounter, it is associated with the unwashed and the violent.

Anonymous university lecturer, quoted in Janet Menzies, Investigation of Attitudes to Scots and Glaswegian Dialect Among Secondary School Pupils *(1975)*

Greitand doun in Gallowa
mar bu dual don gallow breid
    (the habit of yon gallows breed)
a' dranndail is ag cainntearachd
    (muttering and deedling, piper-like)
le my trechour tung, gun teagamh
    (with my traitor tongue, doubtless)
that hes tane ane hyland strynd.
    (that has taken a Highland twist)
    William Neill (1922–2010), De A Thug Ort Sgriobhadh Ghaidhlig? (*What Made You Write in Gaelic?*)

I speak just the fine English now,
My own ways left behind;
The good schoolmaster taught me how;
they purified my mind
from the errors of any kind.
William Neill, Dh' fhalbh sin is tha 'inig seo
(*That's Gone and This Has Come*)

Anywhere in the world where there's dying language, the
neighbours say the people are lazy and prone to drink.
Sir Iain Noble (1935–2010), quoted in Kenneth Roy,
Conversations in a Small Country (*1989*)

A conscientious Chinaman who contemplated a thesis on the
literary history of Scotland would have no doubt as to his
procedure: 'I will learn a little Gaelic, and read all I can find
about Gaelic literature …' He would be rather mystified when
he found that historians of Scotland and its literature had
known and cared as much about Gaelic as about Chinese.
William Power (1873–1953), Literature and Oatmeal

There is no greater impediment to the advancement of
knowledge than the ambiguity of words.
Thomas Reid (1710–1796), Essays on the Intellectual
Powers of Man

We've words afouth, that we can ca' our ain,
Tho' frae them now my childer sair refrain.
Alexander Ross (1699–1784), Helenore

Ae day laest ouk, whin I was gaen t' da sola, I met wir
skülmaister. I gees him da time o da day, an' speaks back
an' fore, dan he says to me, 'Fat's yer wee bit loonie deein',
that he's nae been at skool syne Monday week?' Noo sir,
haed I been askin' dis question I wid hae said, 'What's your
peerie boy düin' 'at he's no been at skül frae last
Moninday?' … we pay dem fur laernin' bairns English, no
fur unlearnin' wir Shetlan' speech.'
Shetland Times, '*Recollections of the Past*' (*November 1880*)

He who loses his language loses his world.
Iain Crichton Smith (1928–1998), Shall Gaelic Die?

Man is a creature who lives not by bread alone, but
principally by catchwords.
Robert Louis Stevenson (1850–1894)

'Lallans' – a synthesised Burnsian esperanto; 'Plastic Scots'
its enemies called it.
John Sutherland, The Times Literary Supplement
(August 1998)

Many people think that Scots possesses a rich vocabulary,
but this is a view not wholly borne out by a close
examination ... It is as if the Doric had been invented by a
cabal of scandal-mongering beldams, aided by a council of
observant gamekeepers.
George Malcolm Thomson (1899–1996),
The Rediscovery of Scotland

I am fascinated and frightened by the power and danger of
words, which are so often grave obstacles to full honesty of
thought.
Sir Robert Watson-Watt (1892–1973), Three Steps to Victory

Work and Leisure

If it wasna for the weavers, whit wad we do?
We wadna hae claes made o' oor woo',
We wadna hae a cloot, neither black nor blue,
If it wasna for the wark o' the weavers.
Traditional, The Wark o' the Weavers

O' a' the trades that I do ken,
The beggin' is the best,
For when a beggar's weary,
He can aye sit doon an' rest.
Traditional, Tae the Beggin' I Will Go

Nothing is really work unless you would rather be doing something else.
Sir J.M. Barrie (1860–1937)

A man willing to work, and unable to find work, is perhaps the saddest sight that fortune's inequality exhibits under this sun.
Thomas Carlyle (1795–1881), Chartism

Rest is for the dead.
Thomas Carlyle, quoted by J. A. Froude, Life of Carlyle: The First Forty Years

It's just the power of some to be a boss,
And the bally power of others to be bossed.
John Davidson (1857–1909), Thirty Bob a Week

Work and play! Work and play!
The order of the universe.
John Davidson, Piper, Play

… with thy neichbours gladly lend and borrow;
His chance tonight, it may be thine tomorrow.
William Dunbar (c.1460–c.1520), No Treasure without Gladness

I'm far owre weill to wark the day.
Robert Garioch (Robert Garioch Sutherland, 1908–1981), Owre Weill

Oh, it's nice to get up in the mornin'
And nicer to stay in bed.
Sir Harry Lauder (1870–1950)

You would not think any duty small
If you yourself were great.
George Macdonald (1824–1905), Willie's Question

Work, eh. What a stupid way to earn a living.
Ian Pattison (1950–), 'At the Job Centre', from
Rab C. Nesbitt: The Scripts (*1990*)

'No-one has ever said it,' observed Lady Caroline, 'but how painfully true it is that the poor have us always with them!'
Saki (H.H. Munro, 1870–1916)

I consider the capacity to labour as part of the happiness I have enjoyed.
Sir Walter Scott (1771–1832) quoted in Lockhart's Life of Scott

I was not long, however, in making the grand discovery, that in order to enjoy leisure, it is absolutely necessary it should be preceded by occupation.
Sir Walter Scott, Introductory Epistle to The Monastery

Our business in this world is not to succeed, but to continue to fail, in good spirits.
Robert Louis Stevenson (1850–1894)

There is no duty we so much under-rate as the duty of being happy.
Robert Louis Stevenson, An Apology for Idlers

'Ye'll need tae gie us a bung though Gav. Ah'm fuckin brassic until this rent cheque hits the mat the morn.'
Irvine Welsh (1957–), Trainspotting

Writers and Readers

There is no mood to which a man may not administer the appropriate medicine at the cost of reaching down a volume from his bookshelf.
A.J. Balfour (1848–1930), Essays and Addresses

Biography should be written by an acute enemy.
  A.J. Balfour, quoted in The Observer, *1927*

The worst books make the best films.
  Iain Banks (1954–2013)

Still am I besy bokes assemblynge
For to have plenty it is a pleasant thynge
In my conceyt and to have them ay in honde
But what they mene do I nat understonde
  Alexander Barclay (c.1475–1552),
  The Shyp of Folys of the Worlde

It is all very well to be able to write books, but can you
waggle your ears?
  Sir J.M. Barrie (1860–1937), letter to H.G. Wells

I remember being asked by two maiden ladies about the
time I left the university, what I was to be, and when I
replied brazenly, 'An Author,' they flung up their hands,
and one exclaimed reproachfully, 'And you an MA!'
  Sir J.M. Barrie, Margaret Ogilvy

For several days after my first book was published, I carried
it about in my pocket, and took surreptitious peeps at it to
make sure that the ink had not faded.
  Sir J.M. Barrie, speech to the Critics' Circle, 1920

… copulation is a sweet and necessary act … it is like
defecation, an exceedingly interesting process; but it is
much better described in physiological textbooks than in all
the works of all the novelists ancient and modern who have
ever existed.
  James Bridie (Osborne Henry Mavor, 1888–1951),
  letter to Neil Gunn, January 1932

Critics! appall'd I venture on the name,
Those cut-throat bandits on the path of fame.
  Robert Burns (1759–1796)s, On Critics

Gie me ae spark o' Nature's fire,
That's a' the learning I desire;
Then, tho' I drudge thro' dub and mire
At pleugh or cart,
My Muse, tho' hamely in attire,
May touch the heart.
    Robert Burns, Epistle to J. Lapraik

Quelle vie! Let no woman who values peace of soul ever
dream of marrying an author!
    Jane Welsh Carlyle (1801–1866), letter to John Sterling, 1837

If a book come from the heart, it will contrive to reach
other hearts; all art and authorcraft are of small amount to
that.
    Thomas Carlyle (1795–1881), On Heroes, Hero-Worship,
    and the Heroic in History.

… a well-written life is almost as rare as a well-spent one
    Thomas Carlyle, Essays, *on Jean Paul Richter*

Beis weill advisit my werk or ye reprief;
Consider it warely, read ofter than anis,
Weill, at ane blenk, slee poetry nocht ta'en is.
    Gavin Douglas (1475–1522), Prologue to the Aeneid

So me behovit whilom, or than be dumb,
Some bastard Latin, French or Inglis use,
Where scant were Scottis; I had na other choiss.
    Gavin Douglas, Prologue to the Aeneid

A man should keep his little brain attic stocked with all the
furniture that he is likely to use, and the rest he can put
away in the lumber room of his library, where he can get it
if he wants it.
    Sir Arthur Conan Doyle (1859–1930),
    The Adventures of Sherlock Holmes

Poetry and prayer are very similar.
Carol Ann Duffy (1955–)

On Waterloo's ensanguined plain
Lie tens of thousands of the slain,
But none by sabre or by shot
Fell half so flat as Walter Scott.
Thomas, Lord Erskine (1750–1823), on Scott's
The Field of Waterloo

I cannot endure that man's writing – his vulgarity beats print.
Susan Ferrier (1782–1854), quoted by James Irvine in his Introduction to The Inheritance *(1984), on John Galt*

The best a writer writes is Beautiful
He should ignore the mad and dutiful.
Ian Hamilton Finlay (1925–1996), The Writer and Beauty

Nobody told me Shakespeare would be a thrill.
Janice Galloway (1955–), All Made Up

the pleasure of creating something where nothing had been.
Janice Galloway, All Made Up

I am so horrified by all the dirty little cruelties and bestialities that I would feel the lowest type of skunk if I didn't shout the horror of them from the rooftops. Of course I shout too loudly.
Lewis Grassic Gibbon (James Leslie Mitchell, 1901–1935), letter quoted in Helen B. Cruickshank, Octobiography

For Mora
At long last, a book by her brother which will not make her blush.
Alasdair Gray (1934–2019), Dedication of
The Fall of Kelvin Walker

The Scottish poets all felt competent to teach the art of
government to their rulers
    M.M. Gray, Scottish Poetry from Barbour to James VI
    (*1935*)

I can't write a play unless I have a question I can't answer.
    David Greig (1969–), BBC 'Belief' interview

we're very lucky – we don't have Shakespeare – you know
we don't have … anybody hanging over us, who we have to
do.
    David Greig, BBC 'Belief' interview

I mend the fire, and beikit me about,
Then took ane drink my spreitis to comfort,
And armit me weill fra the cauld thereout;
To cut the winter nicht and mak it short,
I took ane quair, and left all other sport
    Robert Henryson (c.1425–c.1500),
    The Testament of Cresseid

Never literary attempt was more unfortunate than my
Treatise of Human Nature. It fell dead-born from the press.
    David Hume (1711–1776), My Own Life

She read the manuscript of her first novel, Marriage, to her
father, behind the cover of a screen that he could not see
what she was reading. He told her 'It was the best book you
have ever brought me.' He considered her assertion that it
was written by a woman as 'nonsense', and then she
confessed that it was her own work.
    James Irvine, Introduction to The Inheritance *by Susan
    Ferrier (1782–1854)*

Och, I wish you hadn't come right now,
You've put me off my balance:
I was just translating my last wee poem
Into the dear old Lallans.
    Alan Jackson (1938–), A Scotch Poet Speaks

Often the least important parts of a book are the ones you remember, which means that its meaning often lies in the bits you forget.
   Robin Jenkins (1912–1992), quoted by Brian Morton in Scottish Review of Books, *vol 1, no. 3, 2005*

With a yell of triumph he finishes the great work;
He slumps back in his seat, exhausted but happy;
Idly, he fingers through it, and reads the very first lines;
Little by little the smile disappears from his face.
   Frank Kuppner (1951–),
   A Bad Day for the Sung Dynasty

Few books today are forgivable.
   R.D. Laing (1927–1989), The Politics of Experience

Authors and uncaptured criminals are the only people free from routine.
   Eric Linklater (1899–1974), Poet's Pub

Our principal writers have nearly all been fortunate in escaping regular education.
   Hugh MacDiarmid (C.M. Grieve, 1892–1978), quoted in The Observer

It seems fatal to write a Scottish novel of promise!
   Hugh Macdiarmid, The Raucle Tongue, *vol 2*

Are my poems spoken in the factories and fields,
In the streets o' the toon?
Gin they're no', then I'm failin' to doe
What I ocht to ha' dune.
   Hugh MacDiarmid (C.M. Grieve, 1892–1978), Second Hymn to Lenin

A Scottish poet maun assume
The burden o' his people's doom,
And dee to brak' their livin' tomb.
   Hugh MacDiarmid, A Drunk Man Looks at the Thistle

The essential beginning of all national uprisings is that poets should believe.
  A.G. Macdonell (1895–1941), My Scotland

I do think the whole climate for writers these days is so vulgar. It's all so money-led. I hate going into book shops and seeing, you know, the Top Ten Bestsellers, a sort of self-fulfilling prophecy. I just find the whole thing so vulgar.
  Shena Mackay (1944–), quoted in The Guardian, *10 September 1999*

The Kailyard School mortgaged Scottish literature to indignity.
  Compton Mackenzie (1883–1972), Literature in My Time

I know the sharp bitterness of the spirit
better than the swift joy of the heart.
  Sorley Maclean (1911–1996), 'When I Speak of the Face'
  (An Uair a Labhras Mi Mu Aodann)

With the birth of each child you lose two novels.
  Candia MacWilliam (1957–), quoted in The Guardian, *1993*

Men of sorrow, and acquainted with Grieve
  Edwin Muir (1887–1959), quoted in Karl Miller,
  Memoirs of a Modern Scotland (1970), *on Scottish writers of the 1930s*

Every critic in the town
Runs the minor poet down;
Every critic – don't you know it!
Is himself a minor poet.
  Robert F. Murray (1863–1894)

I knew the game was up for me the day
I stood before my father's corpse and thought
If I can't get a poem out of this ...
  Don Paterson (1963–)

Writers can redeeem a wasted day in two minutes; alas this knowledge leads them to waste their day like no-one else.
Don Paterson

They say I'm only a poet,
Whose fate is as dead as my verse
(His father's a packman, you know it;
His father, in turn, couldn't boast).
They'd take a good field and plough it.
I can cut better poems than most.
William Ross (1762–1790), Oran Gaoil (*Love Song*),
translated by Iain Crichton Smith

I have seen his pen gang as fast ower the paper, as ever it did ower the water when it was in the grey goose's wing.
Sir Walter Scott (1771–1832), The Heart of Midlothian

Please return this book: I find that though many of my friends are poor arithmeticians, they are nearly all good book-keepers.
Bookmark alleged to belong to Sir Walter Scott

Style, after all, rather than thought, is the immortal thing in literature.
Alexander Smith (1830–1867), Dreamthorp

The skin of a man of letters is peculiarly sensitive to the bite of the critical mosquito, and he lives in a climate in which such mosquitoes swarm. He is seldom stabbed to the heart – he is often killed by pinpricks.
Alexander Smith, Dreamthorp

We'd never expect to understand a piece of music on one listen, but we tend to believe we've read a book after reading it just once.
Ali Smith (1962–), Artful

Poetry drives its lines into her forehead
like an angled plough across a bare field.
>   *Iain Crichton Smith (1928–1998)*, A Young Highland
>   Girl studying Poetry

Every person of importance ought to write his own
memoirs, provided he has honesty enough to tell the truth.
>   *Tobias Smollett (1721–1771)*

There are mair sangs that bide unsung
nor aa that hae been wrocht.
>   *William Soutar (1898–1943)*, The Makar

There is but one art – to omit! O if I knew how to omit, I
would ask no other knowledge.
>   *Robert Louis Stevenson (1850–1894),*
>   *Letter to R.A.M. Stevenson (1883)*

The Scots are incapable of considering their literary
geniuses purely as writers or artists. They must be either an
excuse for a glass or a text for the next sermon.
>   *George Malcolm Thomson, (1899–1996)*, Caledonia

Give a man a pipe he can smoke,
Give a man a book he can read:
And his home is bright with a calm delight,
Though the room be poor indeed.
>   *James Thomson (1834–1882)*, Sunday Up the River

Oh! If by any unfortunate chance I should happen to die,
In a French field of turnips or radishes I'll lie.
But thinking of it as really Scottish all the time,
Because my patriotic body will impart goodness to the slime.
>   *J.Y. Watson*, A Pastiche of Rupert Brooke in the style of
>   William McGonagall (*prize-winner in a parody
>   competition, 1950s*)

I enjoy the freedom of the blank page.
>   *Irvine Welsh (1957–)*

Youth and Age

Welcome eild, for youth is gone.
  Anonymous, Welcome Eild

I'm not young enough to know everything.
  Sir J.M. Barrie (1860–1937), The Admirable Crichton

An' O for ane an' twenty, Tam!
And hey, sweet ane an' twenty, Tam!
I'll learn my kin a rattlin sang,
An' I saw ane an' twenty, Tam
  Robert Burns (1759–1796), O For Ane An' Twenty, Tam

The dreams of age are deeper than the dreams of youth,
because the dreams of youth are sharp and thin like new
wine, and the dreams of age are rich and fragrant, and
tinged with tragic knowledge.
  H.J. Cameron (1873–1932), Under the Diamond

The auld wife sat ayont her man,
But nae auld carle saw she;
And, gin he keekit owre at her,
An auld wife saw na he.
Wi tousy head a cottar lad
Sat in the auld man's place,
And glowered, tongue-tackit, at the stars
That lauched in Jeanie's face.
  A.M. Davidson (1897–1979), Auld Fowk

I wes in yowth on nureis knee
Dandely, Bischop, dandely;
And quhen that ege now dois me greif,
Ane simple vicar I can nocht be.
  William Dunbar (c.1460–c.1520), To the King

Worldly prudence is very suitable at seventy, but at seventeen it is absolutely disgusting.

Susan Ferrier (1782–1854), Letter to Walter Ferrier, in J. A. Doyle, Memoir and Correspondence of Susan Ferrier (*1898*)

Eild comes owre me like a yoke on my craig

George Campbell Hay (1915–1984), The Auld Hunter, *translated from Gaelic by Hugh MacDiarmid*

The moir of ege the nerrer hevynis bliss.

Robert Henryson (c.1425–1500), The Praise of Age

It's frightening to get old anyway, but if your looks were the cornerstone of your life, well, it would be very difficult.

Lulu (Lulu Kennedy-Cairns, 1948–)

If you think you're old, you'll feel old.

Lulu

Our hearts are young 'neath wrinkled rind:
Life's more amusing than we thought.

Andrew Lang (1844–1912), Ballade of Middle Age

Youth having passed, there is nothing to lose but memory.

George Macdonald (1824–1905), Fifty Years of Freethought

Age is not all decay; it is the ripening, the swelling, of the fresh life within, that withers and bursts the husk.

George Macdonald, The Marquis of Lossie

Young people grow up today in a society of deep-set gloom and despondency. They live in a glitz, glam and celeb culture where superficiality and owning more things seems the order of the day, unsustainable materialism, and where greed, lack of responsibility and respect are constant reminders of a hopeless decline in our values and vision.

Henry McLeish (1948–), Holyrood *magazine, October 2011*

After a certain age all of us, good and bad, are guilt-stricken because of powers within us which have never been realised; because, in other words, we are not what we should be.
Edwin Muir (1887–1959), Autobiography

My heart's still light, albeit my locks be grey.
Allan Ramsay (1686–1758), The Gentle Shepherd

My Peggy is a young thing,
And I'm nae very auld
Allan Ramsay, The Waukin' o' the Fauld

Be sure ye dinna quit the grip
Of ilka joy, when ye are young,
Before auld age your vitals nip,
And lay ye twa-fold o'er a rung.
Allan Ramsay, Miscellany

All sorts of allowances are made for the illusions of youth; and none, or almost none, for the disenchantments of age.
Robert Louis Stevenson (1850–1894), Virginibus Puerisque

Old and young, we are all on our last cruise.
Robert Louis Stevenson, Virginibus Puerisque

For God's sake give me the young man who has brains enough to make a fool of himself.
Robert Louis Stevenson, Virginibus Puerisque

Index of Persons Quoted

Aberdein, John 41
Adam, Robert 97
Ainslie, Hew 93
Alexander, Sir William 118
Allan, John R. 113
Alison, Sir Archibald 97
Anderson, Alexander 23
Angus, Marion 58, 93, 97
Annand, J.K 13, 58
Arbuthnot, John 74
Armstrong, John 113
Ascherson, Neal 8
Ayton, Sir Robert 59, 118
Aytoun, W.E. 71
Baillie, Joanna 135
Baillie, Robert 97
Baird, John Logie 79
Balfour, A.J. 80, 87, 145, 146
Banks, Iain 41, 146
Bannerman, J.M. 28
Barbour, John 107, 130
Barclay, Alexander 47, 146
Barclay, John 66
Barclay, William 80, 118
Barrie, Sir J.M. 8, 17, 36, 41, 62, 71, 87, 98, 118, 135, 144, 146, 154
Belhaven, Lord 80, 107
Bell, E.T. 87
Bell, J.H.B. 67
Bell, Joseph 66
Bermant, Chaim 74
Birnie, Patrick 13
Black, William 108
Blackhall, Sheena 94
Blackie, John Stuart 87, 135
Blind Harry 101
Bold, Alan 108
Bonar, Horatius 31
Boswell, James 28, 98, 126
Boyd, Mark Alexander 59
Boyd, William 135
Boyle, Frankie 41, 80, 118, 126
Braxfield, Lord 56, 62
Bridie, James 146
Brougham, Lord 34, 87, 105
Brown, Arnold 98
Brown, George Mackay 13, 17, 39, 91, 94, 135
Brown, Gordon 26, 74
Brown, Hamish 68
Brown, Ivor 119, 136
Brown, Jim 126
Brown, John 41, 94

Bruce, George 69
Bruce of Kinnaird, Robert 31
Buchan, John 8, 71, 74, 80, 113
Buchan, Tom 53
Buchanan, George 9, 136
Burnet, Gilbert 98
Burns, Robert 9, 13, 18, 21, 26, 28, 31, 41, 42, 56, 59, 62, 63, 71, 80, 94, 98, 108, 119, 125, 130, 136, 146, 147, 154
Burnside, John 9
Busby, Sir Matt 9
Byrne, David 69, 119
Byron, Lord 21
Caie, J.M. 14
Cairncross, Sir Alexander 88
Calder, Ritchie 88
Calgacus 50
Cameron, H.J. 154
Cameron, Richard 80
Campbell, Donald 94
Campbell, James 136
Campbell, Sir Colin 131
Campbell, Thomas 31, 51, 81, 119, 125
Campbell-Bannerman, Sir Henry 131
Cargill, Donald 81
Carlyle, Alexander 99
Carlyle, Jane Welsh 9, 47, 66, 147
Carlyle, Thomas 9, 10, 22, 28, 34, 42, 47, 53, 63, 81, 99, 136, 144, 147
Carnegie, Andrew 26, 99
Carswell, Catherine 22, 81
Carswell, John 137
Christie, J.R. 53, 108
Cockburn, Alison 51
Cockburn, Henry Thomas 31, 63, 99, 126
Cockburn, Robin 42
Cocker, W.D. 81
Committee of the SPCK 137
Connery, Sir Sean 99
Connolly, Sir Billy 10, 42, 66, 94, 108
Corrie, Joe 119
'Cosgrove, Mrs Alice' 113
Crawford, Robert 137
Crockett, S.R. 42, 88
Cunningham, Allan 53, 91, 108
Curran, James 115
Cutler, Ivor 34
Daiches, David 137

Darling, Sir Frank Fraser 53, 94
Darling, William Y. 14
Davidson, A.M. 137, 154
Davidson, John 10, 14, 144
Denholm, T. S. 126
Dewar, Donald 42, 99
Dewar, James 66, 74
Dickson, David 81
Docherty, Tommy 114
Donaldson, Margaret C. 34
Douglas, Gavin 53, 95, 138, 147
Douglas, George 18, 100
Douglas, Norman 42, 47, 74
Douglas, T.L. 119
Douglas, William 59
Doyle, Sir Arthur Conan 88, 147
Drummond, Henry 10, 81
Drummond, William 60, 68, 119
Duffy, Carol Ann 74, 120, 148
Dunbar, William 32, 38, 51, 95, 100, 120, 144, 154
Dundee, Lord 42
Dundee, Viscount 109
Dunn, Douglas 34
Elliott, Jane 51
Elliott, Walter 72
Erskine, Henry 109
Erskine, Lord 148
Erskine, Ruaraidh 82
Ewen, John 92
Ewing, Winnie 20, 75
Faichney, William 82
Ferguson, Adam 26
Ferguson, James 23
Ferguson, John 43
Fergusson, Robert 28, 43, 95
Ferrie, Hugh 114
Ferrier, Susan 36, 148, 155
Finlay, Ian Hamilton 69, 95, 120, 148
Fleming, Marjory 82, 100
Fleming, Sir Alexander 88
Fletcher, Andrew 56, 109
Forbes, Bertie Charles 10
Fordun, John 120
Fraser, G.S. 120, 138
Fraser, George Macdonald 114, 120
Frazer, Sir James 36
Fyffe, Will 58
Galloway, Janice 10, 23, 100, 148
Galt, John 32, 100
Gardner, Robert 114
Garioch, Robert 114, 144
Garry, Flora 95
Geddes, Alexander 138
Geddes, Jenny 82
Geddes, Sir Patrick 54, 63
Geikie, Sir Archibald 35, 127

Gibbon, Lewis Grassic, 10, 28, 43, 54, 60, 101, 138, 148
Goldie, Annabel 75
Gordon, Seton 69
Graham, H. Grey, 10
Graham, R.B. Cunninghame 32, 75
Graham, W.S. 63, 138
Grahame, Kenneth 14, 47
Grant, Ann 72
Grant, I.F. 39
Gray, Alasdair 23, 28, 35, 127, 148
Gray, Sir Alexander 54
Gray, M.M. 149
Greig, David 139, 149
Gunn, Neil 43, 92, 109
Hagan, Harry 14
Haig, Earl 131
Haldane, J.B.S. 66, 82, 88, 139
Haliburton, Hugh 139
Hamilton, Ian 56
Hamilton, Janet 43, 54
Hamilton, John 120
Hanley, Cliff 109
Hardie, James Keir 101
Harvie, Christopher 75, 101, 139
Hay, George Campbell 155
Hay, Ian 35
Hedderwick, James 120
Henderson, Hamish 75, 131
Henryson, Robert 11, 43, 51, 101, 149, 155
Hogg, James 23, 39, 54, 60, 82, 102, 121, 125, 139
Horne, John 72
Home, Lord, 115
Hume, Alexander 32
Hume, David 32, 47, 48, 63, 75, 82, 83, 88, 102, .149
Hutcheson, Francis 10
Hutton, James 89
Imlach, Hamish 60
Irvine, James 149
Jackson, Alan 102, 149
Jacob, Violet 54, 64, 95, 121
James I 39, 60
James V 121
James VI 36, 67, 75, 139
Jamie, Kathleen 95
Jenkins, Robin 29, 150
Johnston, Ellen 75
Johnston, Tom 26, 76, 102
Johnstone, Henry 15, 95
Kay, Jackie 60, 102, 139
Keith, Sir Arthur 72, 83, 131
Kelman, James 18, 24, 36, 43, 70, 76
Kelvin, Lord 67, 83, 89
Kennaway, James 72

Kennedy, Helena 83
Kennedy, Walter 70
Kesson, Jessie 64
Knox, John 64, 83
Kuppner, Frank 102, 150
Laing, R.D. 24, 67, 150
Lang, Andrew 76, 89, 109, 115, 155
Lauder, Sir Harry 11, 144
Law, Andrew Bonar 76, 130
Lee, Jennie 24
Lee, Joseph 131
Leonard, Tom 140
Leyden, Dr John 140
Liddell, Eric H. 115
Lindsay, Maurice 110, 121, 140
Lindsay, Sir David 44, 56, 72, 102
Lingard, Joan 37
Linklater, Eric 44, 102, 115, 150
Livingstone, David 11
Lochhead, Liz 64, 121
Logan, Jimmy 44
Lulu 155
Lynch, Michael 72
Lyndsay, John 83
Lyte, Henry Francis 84
Macari, Lou 115
McCabe, Brian 127
MacCaig, Norman 11, 15, 48, 92, 93, 96, 103, 127
MacCodrum, John 29
MacCulloch, J.A. 44
McDermid, Val 64
MacDiarmid, Hugh 15, 20, 22, 37, 55, 57, 64, 73, 76, 84, 110, 121, 131, 140, 150
Macdonald, George 11, 15, 51, 84, 92, 121, 144, 155
Macdonald, Iain Lòm 76
MacDonald, Ronald 132
Macdonell, A.G. 110, 151
MacGillivray, Pittendrigh 20
McGrath, John 26
McHarg, Alastair 116
McIlvanney, Hugh 116
McIlvanney, William 110
MacIntyre, Duncan Bàn 140
Mackay, Charles 22, .140
McKay, D.M. 29
McKay, John 116
Mackay, Shena 151
McKean, Charles 18
Mackenzie, Agnes Mure 110
Mackenzie, Compton 37, 151
Mackenzie, Murdo 33
Mackenzie, R.F. 35
Mackenzie, Sir George 103, 141
Mackie, Alastair 24, 37, 121

Mackintosh, E.A. 132
Mackintosh, Charles Rennie 11, 18
Mackintosh, Sir James 11, 77
McLean, Jim 116
Maclean, John 77, 132
Maclean, Sorley 55, 73, 110, 141, 151
McLeish, Henry 155
MacLennan, Murdoch 132
MacLeod, Fiona 39, 55, 92, 96, 103
MacLeod, Kenneth
Macleod, Norman 52, 84, 92
MacMillan, Sir James 70
Macnab, The 133
McNaughtan, Adam 127
McNeill, F. Marian 44
Macpherson, James 52
Macpherson, Mary 57
Macquarie, Lachlan 103
MacWilliam, Candia 110, 151
Maitland, Sir Richard 48, 52, 122
Mansfield, Lord 57
Manson, Sir Patrick 89
Marshall, Bruce 64, 141
Martin, Jim 77
Matheson, George 84
Maxwell, James Clerk 89, 90
Mickle, W.J. 65
Miller, Hugh 122
Miller, William 24
Milne, J.C. 111
Mitchell, Joseph 127
Moffat, Gwen 68
Monro, Harold 16
Montgomerie, Alexander 52
Montgomery, James 16
Montrose, Marquis of 20
Morgan, Edwin 103
Morrison, Grant 24
Morrison, R.F. 44
Muir, Edwin 18, 22, 73, 103, 111, 122, 125, 151, 156
Muir, John 22, 33, 122
Muir, Willa 84
Munro, H.H., see Saki
Munro, Neil 16, 45, 60, 104, 133
Murchison, Sir Roderick 90
Murray, Charles 29, 68, 104, 133
Murray, Chic 11
Murray, George 84
Murray, Robert F. 48, 151
Murray, W.H. 68
Nairn, Tom 110, 116
Nairne, Lady 11, 33, 45, 104
Neill, A.S. 35
Neill, William 16, 141, 142
Nicolson, Alexander 127
Noble, Sir Iain 142

North, Christopher 27, 45, 73, 77
Ogilvie, Will H. 133
Oliphant, Margaret 122
Orr, John Boyd 122
Park, Mungo 48
Paterson, Don 11, 104, 151, 152
Patey, Tom 68
Pattison, Ian 45, 145
Peden, Alexander 65
Perrie, Walter 11
Playfair, John 90
Pollok, Robert 11, 104
Power, William 142
Ramsay, Allan 29, 60, 156
Ramsay, Dean E.B. 45, 84, 104
Ramsay, Gordon 45
Randolph, Agnes 111
Reid, Alastair 16
Reid, John Macnair 85
Reid, Sir Bob 116
Reid, Thomas 142
Reith, Lord 77, 105
Rendall, Robert 33, 111
Renwick, James 77, 111
Rifkind, Sir Malcolm 77, 123
Roberton, Sir Hugh S. 125
Robertson, John M. 45, 85
Robertson, R. 92
Rodger, Alexander 11
Roper, Tony 111
Ross, Alexander 142
Ross, Sir Ronald 90
Ross, William 152
Rush, Christopher 123
Rutherford, Samuel 85
Saki 12, 29, 35, 85, 145
Salmond, Alex 77, 78
Scott, Alexander 61
Scott, Sir Walter 21, 25, 30, 48, 57,
    61, 65, 68, 93, 105, 111, 112, 123,
    133, 145, 152
Scott, Tom 46, 85, 105
Scott, Wat 133
Scott, William Bell 39
Sempill, Francis 46, 48, 70
SFA Disciplinary Committee 114
Shankly, Bill 116, 117
Shepherd, Nan 55, 68, 105
Shetland Times 142
Shields, Alexander 78
Sillars, Jim 27, 112
Simpson, Sir James Young 90
Sinclair, Sir John 30
Skinner, John 16
Slessor, Catherine 19
Slessor, Mary 83
Smeaton, John 78

Smiles, Samuel 12
Smith, Adam 27, 91, 105, 134
Smith, Alexander 105, 152
Smith, Ali 152
Smith, Iain Crichton 55, 65, 93, 112,
    123, 128, 143, 153
Smith, Mark R. 70
Smith, Sydney Goodsir 134
Smith, W. Gordon 30, 117, 134
Smith, William Robertson 85
Smollett, Tobias 12, 61, 67, 153
Somerville, Mary 85
Sorley, C.H. 123, 134
Souness, Graeme 117
Soutar, William 25, 40, 46, 61, 67,
    73, 78, 96, 123, 134, 153
Spark, Muriel 12, 25, 35, 106
Spence, Lewis 19
Stein, Jock 117
Stevenson, Robert Louis 17, 19, 21,
    25, 27, 33, 37, 40, 49, 65, 86, 93,
    96, 106, 123, 128, 134,
    143, 145, 153, 156
Stewart, Al 13, 106
Stewart, Dugald 124
Stewart, Sir James 86
Stirling Prize Judges 19
Strang, Sandy 117
Strange, Lady 37
Stuart, Prince Charles Edward 21, 49
Sturgeon, Nicola 65, 79
Sutherland, John 143
Tannahill, Robert 106
Thompson, Sir D'Arcy Wentworth
    17, 91
Thomson, Derick 52
Thomson, George Malcolm 143, 153
Thomson, James (b.1700) 33, 36, 96
Thomson, James (b.1834) 33, 34,
    49, 86, 124, 128, 153
Thomson, Thomas 124
Vettese, Raymond 86
Watson, J.Y. 153
Watson-Watt, Sir Robert 106, 112,
    143
Watt, James 91
Weir, Judith 71
Welsh, Irvine 37, 65, 67, 74, 106,
    145, 153
Whyte-Melville, George 13, 61, 86
Wilkie, Sir David 19
Williamson, Roy 112
Wingate, Walter 124, 128
Wood, Alex 25
Young, Andrew 17, 55, 69, 86, 96
Young, Angus 71
Young, Douglas 21